Funda
pre

Bonhoffer
p 44

Get UNSTUCK
from FUNDAMENTALISM

A Spiritual Journey

"*This book clearly illustrates how any limiting and rigid beliefs–religious or otherwise–can cause divisiveness and deep misunderstanding within ourselves, our communities, and our world. Fortunately, Robert Crosby takes us on a thought-provoking spiritual journey toward openness, compassion, and faith without boundaries. Filled with wisdom, fascinating historical references, and even blending in Italy's splendor, this book offers a taste of how to get unstuck, find your essence, and experience the joy that follows. This is a valuable book for anyone who wants to explore new perspectives on what it means to live an authentic and moral life.*"

— **Donald Altman, M.A.,** psychotherapist, former Buddhist monk, and author of *Living Kindness, Meal By Meal, and Art of the Inner Meal.*

"*A deeply affecting, deeply personal faith journey. Highly recommended.*"
— **Rabbi James L. Mirel, D.D.**

"*Crosby's approach is ecumenical, in the widest sense of the word. He still embraces some Christian ideas but blends them with Hindu, Buddhist and Muslim thought, together with healthy doses of psychology and philosophy....*"

— **James B. Recob, Ph.D,** Emeritus Professor of Religion, Otterbein College.

"*This remarkable little volume encourages the authentic celebration of the abundant life Jesus promised. As we embrace the 'Now'--the circumstances and travelling companions of our daily lives--rigid literalism and second-hand indoctrination are 'left behind.'*"

— **Margaret Starbird**, author of *The Woman with the Alabaster Jar, Mary Magdalene, Bride in Exile* and others.

"*... a deceptively ambitious, delightfully written book talks about fundamentalism, placing it within the Christian tradition, analyzing its logic (and illogic) and critiquing its impact on contemporary American politics. But it does much more, offering a life-giving alternative. Enjoyable, clear and 'gettable' from cover to cover...*"

— **Donald S. Williamson, Ph.D,** Past-President of the American Association of Marriage and Family Therapists, former faculty member of the Duke University Divinity School and Baylor College of Medicine and currently a Senior Fellow at the Leadership Institute of Seattle. He is the author of *The Intimacy Paradox.*

Get UNSTUCK
from FUNDAMENTALISM

A Spiritual Journey

By Robert Parson Crosby

ISBN: 0-9776900-0-8

MAY THIS BOOK BE A HELPFUL GUIDE THROUGH THE FOG OF LIFE.

To my grandchildren
Jake, Meggan, Jennifer, Stacia, Parson, Dao, Willow, Sarah, Alexa,
Celeste, Melody, Gigi, Joy, Matteo.

My great-grandchild
Madelynn Amber
and those yet to be born and their children.

God-granddaughter in Kiev, Ukraine
Katorina (Katya)

Grand-nieces and nephew
Ben, Kate, Paige, Jennifer

You are accepted, just as you are!

Buddhist 9th century

ACKNOWLEDGEMENTS

*M*y friend and financial advisor, Ron Reynolds, suggested in June 2004 that I write another book while in Italy, because he believed that I still had something to say and I'm sure he had financial advantages in mind. Ours is one of those rare relationships where, while we connect at a "spirit" level and often differ at a conceptual level, we continue to talk openly and to deeply respect each other.

One hundred years earlier (June 1904), my grandfather, George Britton McClellan Erwin, began writing his book, "Twenty Pathways Leading to Judgment." His book and this book of mine are very different in certain basic assumptions. However, at the "spirit" level, I remain inspired by him and connected to him. I love him deeply.

From Italy, I brought handwritten scribbles which, when transcribed were 137 pages in length. Thanks to Josh Malle of Globe Secretariat for his amazing patience and skill in turning the rough documents into excellent print. Later, Amy Wyland skillfully helped me through a final editing process.

After several edits, but while the book was still a series of 72 essays, I found 14 readers who read and commented on all or part of the book. One of them, my son Chris Crosby, helped me to transform the book from a series of essays to its present format of sections and chapters.

The other 13 readers include two of my grandchildren, Dao and Parson Crosby, whose 15-year-old perspective was important for me to hear. The others were: James Brock, David Crosby, Barbara Delauter, Jim Hinde, Tim Hoffman, Ted Hunter, Jason Marvin, Siobhan McComb, Carl Milton, Scott Smith, and Jim Sullivan. My special neighbor, Giulio di Furia, rescued me from Italian language errors.

With feedback from my readers, I then turned my next editing effort over to Mary Anne Owens, whose help in several of my previous books had been invaluable. Only I can realize how much she aided me in the flow and in the grammar of this book. Thank you, Mary Anne.

After this editing, two other readers, Bruce and Gina Anderson, wrote several pages of thoughtful critique. Also, thanks to Brenda Kerr for her insightful comments.

Rei Hanscomb gifted me with a comprehensive proofing. I am deeply grateful.

My chief supporter and critic (and wife), Patricia, once again was there for me, not only during the daily writing in Italy but during the seven months of editing, editing and editing.

Thank you, Gayle Goldman, for your help in layout, design, production, and...and...and... She is indeed an artist. Gayle has helped me in most of my other books, also.

A special thanks to my friend and long time colleague Denny Minno. While we are quite compatible in thought about most of what's in this book, we do disagree profoundly on certain issues. His critique was not only unusually thorough, but also given in the full spirit of honest dialogue. That kind of colleagueship is all too rare.

The photo of the author on the front cover is by Doug Smith.

And finally, thanks to Ricardo at Antica Macelleria, the butcher shop in Panzana, for the photo used in Chapter Eleven and the workshop participant from the Alcoa Fusina plant near Venice for the sketch on page 164.

GET UNSTUCK FROM FUNDAMENTALISM
A Spiritual Journey
TABLE OF CONTENTS

PREFACE
Finding the Jewel Within

I saw this phrase in a dream and nearly used it as my title. It speaks to me of our essential obligation in life—to find our core, the jewel we each are, the brilliant, star-like center of our being.

This has been my own journey now for 77 years. I have learned a few things in this time and join you as a fellow traveler who has a few more miles on my clock than most. This is not a scholarly volume; rather, I wish to write as simply as I can about life and faith and about my "real world" travels in Italy, where so many of these ideas gained focus and demanded to be set down in writing.

As is typical of those who approach the Winter of their days, I find myself having extended conversations in my mind with my children, step-children, grandchildren, grand-nieces and nephew, great-grandchild, God-granddaughter in Ukraine and future generations. So, much of what I write here is for them and speaks to how they might go about finding their jewel within.[1]

This journey begins with a breaking away from our origins.

This sounds paradoxical, and I suppose it is. But to move forward, there is much we need to leave behind. Specifically, getting unstuck from the literalism of our youth is critical to finding the jewel within.

Any kind of literalism is problematic. But the particular type of literalism in which I was raised was Christian. My parents were conservative Protestant Christians, so I grew up in that tradition, and from ages 15 through 18, I was swept up in Fundamentalist Christianity (which I explain in Part Two). Like other children, I

---

[1] Many of the footnotes that appear throughout this book are included to assist these younger readers. Further, I have chosen to forego a scholarly approach to citations and other matters. Instead, I have included a Selected Bibliography at the end of the book that includes most of the books and other material from which I have quoted or which have contributed to my thinking on various subjects.

grew up believing that Jonah literally was swallowed by a whale, that Adam and Eve lived in a garden, and that angels protected children on a regular basis. While I use the term *Christian* literalism, I mean to include all varieties of literalism because, while the focus of my youthful literalistic beliefs were essentially those of fundamentalist Christianity, I believe that any kind of literalism, while normal in childhood, is an impediment to growth in adulthood. And we will only find the jewel within if we can cut loose and get unstuck from literalistic belief systems and secondhand learning.

In the balance of this book, I return often to this basic premise to expand upon it, discover its further implications, and explain and investigate it. So, Part One draws on my mystical side, reaching beyond the common understanding of "faith" and yet claiming simplicity. Part Two is more scholarly, persuasive and autobiographical. Part Three comes, hopefully, from the grandfather with wisdom about a wide spectrum of life's experiences.

While my reference point is Christian literalism, which is the tradition I know best, I read about and talk with others from different traditions. The poetry of Rumi, the Sufi (Islam) poet, has inspired me. I read scriptures of different traditions. So, I write from that tradition which I honor but no longer claim in terms of membership. My spirituality transcends any religion just as my citizenship (though technically I am a U.S. citizen) is universal in spirit. I have cut loose but not *cut off*. Indeed, my spirituality is the most important dimension of my life. The ancient Hindu scripture says, "Truth is One, Sages call it by many names." Believing that, therefore I can embrace many expressions of faith.

It will be clear that some of what follows was inspired while I was in Tuscany during the month of September, 2004. Some reflects moments in Venice and Verona in August. Much could have been written anywhere even though my essay on Christian literalism was inspired during a luncheon conversation with Patricia and a friend, Ted Hunter, at Enoteca Guida in Sansepolcro, Italy. But my great inspiration is the younger members of my family: I want these essays to help them see through the fog that surrounds us and find their own meaning in life and *their* jewel within.

Seattle, Washington

2005

PART ONE: LIFE AND FAITH SIMPLY PUT

The old road to Volpaia

CHAPTER ONE: WHAT IS

Patricia and I have accumulated about six months of living in Venice since 1997. It is magic for us. Jet-lagged on my first day of this recent journey, I was nonetheless delighted to be sitting in Piazza San Marco. The sun was just beginning its ascent over the medieval buildings and towers surrounding the Piazza as I sat outside the centuries-old Caffé Florian.

To my right was the San Marco Basilica, the crown jewel of the city, with its four majestic bronze horses that overlook the Piazza. Arches of gold-backed glass mosaic display scenes of ancient religious figures and cover every inch of the many-domed interior ceiling. Legend has it that St. Mark is buried in the Basilica.

There were few people in the square at this early hour. Even the pigeons, who claim this place as their own, were quiet, and the moment was enriched with clear tones from the bell tower.

"Who am I in this place?" I wondered. "In this city so full of religious icons, what are the boundaries between symbolism and reality? Or are the symbolic and the legendary as real as—or even more real than—anything else?" Actually, I believe that we create reality through our thoughts.

Thoughts are transitory, always passing through. They are impermanent attempts to define reality, but they are always inadequate. What follows is a series of observations, prompted by my early morning musings in the Piazza San Marco, about "what is" because, simply put, one is closest to one's spirituality when one is in touch with reality. Or should I say "reality?" There's one kind of reality that tells us that the sky seems blue, the fire is warm and it's raining outside. There's another kind of "reality" in which we decide that "blue skies" are "shining on me," that I am safe here by the fire and that Mother Nature is watering her plants. I will be talking about this second kind of "reality." Who decides about the impact of those blue skies? How is that done and who does it? Who can define reality for me?

REALITY

How are you?

Good.

And you?

Great! It doesn't cost any more and

After all

I create my internal state.

A Simple Truth ...

The answer is that I must do it ... alone. I am at the center of my universe. I am the only one always in my skin. I am always the one to decide what my sensory impressions mean. The problem is that I may have gotten the idea (1) that it's someone else's job to do this and tell me, or (2) that I decide for myself—and others as well.

Most humans live as if knowledge about the meaning of Life is outside ourselves—as if a priest, guru, rabbi, imam, ascetic or someone else has the answers. They do not. No guru, no scripture, no church, no authority outside myself has the answers for me.

I hold my answer. And any final answer, if there be such, cannot be put into words, because all thoughts are interpretative and impermanent. And ultimately personal.

To go to this freeing place where I am the creator of my meaning, I must release myself from my conditioned secondhand learning—my ego/personality development.

Another Simple Truth …

I am one with all Life, all existence—from the ultimate womb which is existence itself. As a drop of water is one with the ocean, so we (who are 80% water) are one with all life. We only seem different because our ancestors moved to different places and developed different languages, customs, skin color (influenced by their distance from the equator) and religions. These factors are "separators"—so that, for example, while each religion has value, it also separates us.

But since we all come from the same source, the simple truth is one. Billions of years ago there was a primal atom—the original energy. We all come from that source—all creation, everything—is from that womb. Fifty thousand years ago, the ancestors of all humans who now populate the Earth lived in Africa. We are all descendants of San-Bushman. We are all San-Bushman.[2]

We are one, and we are connected. *Tat Tvam Asi!* Thou art that. You are that. These ancient words, written thousands of years ago in Sanskrit, arguably the oldest written language (the Hindu Upanishads are in Sanskrit), signify the deep connection of all energy.

Tat Tvam Asi!

See the beautiful sunset.

Tat Tvam Asi!

Smell the flower.

Tat Tvam Asi!

Taste the water.

Tat Tvam Asi!

Feel the warmth of the sun.

Tat Tvam Asi!

---

2 This story is told in the "Journey of Man" video tracing our DNA history. See the Selected Bibliography for more information.

Touch the bark of the tree.

> *Tat Tvam Asi!*

Hear the waves.

> *Tat Tvam Asi!*

Face the wind.

> *Tat Tvam Asi!*

Could it be

In the vast scheme of things

When all is said and done

That I am you

And you are me,

And each is everyone!

> *Est!*[3]

Tat Tvam Asi is far more than this poem captures. *Tat Tvam Asi* encompasses all energy—all creation. It means that you and I are one with all existence. Most profoundly, it is the basis of compassion, that is, the inner recognition that I am one with you, one with those I have called "enemy"—one with everything!

ONE

The indescribable is existence.

The indescribable is constantly expanding existence.

I am one with the existence.

> Sigh.

> Peace.

---

3 Est is Latin for "This is it."

My Simple Truth

For me, understanding Life is simple. Living it is sometimes quite difficult. *L'Architettura e' semplice, ma la simplicita difficile:* "Architecture is simple, but the simple difficult," says Leonardo da Vinci. Likewise, Life. The *simple* is that we are one with existence— one with all others. We all come from the same source. All is one. Every leaf varies but is still "tree." Every drop of water in the ocean is "ocean."

The *difficult* is that while we are all one, I am not the same as you.

I am unique and I am one. My ego/personality has developed differently from any other, as have my physical characteristics. My ego development is highly influenced by my family, culture, religion and language—that is, by *secondhand learning.*

But I am *not* my ego.

If you want to know what Hell-on-earth is, Hell is to be stuck in one's ego. Hell is to think of one's ego as one's Self. Hell is to think that one's ego, one's personality—and the culture and religion that influenced its development—is the real Self. It is to think that my secondhand learning represents a better, rather than different, culture or religion than does the secondhand learning of others. Nonsense. Secondhand is, after all, secondhand.

The "peace that passeth understanding"[4] is the peace that comes from freeing oneself from Hell and experiencing deeply, that is, beyond understanding, that I am one with all creation. I am one with the creative force (the god/goddess, if you prefer). I am the creator of my truth and the discoverer of my firsthand knowledge of my essence.

At this deepest level of being—at my essence, which came with me as I emerged from the womb—I belong. I am profoundly already accepted, whole, loved and lovely. This is my birthright.

---

[4] This is an ancient Hindu phrase that also appears in the New Testament in reference to Jesus (Philippians 4:7).

There are no hoops to jump through—no right beliefs to accept. Only one intuitive leap is needed—which is for me to accept my belongingness!

It is said that when the Buddha burst from his mother's side he took several steps and said, "See how special am I!" That (says Joseph Campbell[5]) is what every one of us says when we come forth from the womb and cry: "I am special. I, too, am special. I belong. I am loved."

Huang–Po, the ninth century Buddhist priest, says, "Ordinary beings are the Buddha, just as they are." We are loved. No strings attached. It's that simple.

Or, More Simply Put

OM

A sound

No words

The first letter of a most ancient language
(Sanskrit)

OM

Or (more accurately) Aum

The A for my here and now awareness outside self.

The U (oo) for my awareness of my internal
dreaming space.

The M for dreamless sleep—the purifying sleep of
peace.

From which I came into the world

To which I go.

Breathe. Sigh.

Know calmness.

5 See Bibliography

Oм.

Or *The Simplest*

Om

Say "Yes!"

In this and every

Moment

To life!

CHAPTER TWO: EGO AND ESSENCE

*I*n 1977, walking in Bordeaux, I came across an ancient Roman village, near St. Emilion. Ausone, the Roman soldier and poet, settled there in 383. In my journal I wrote:

383 A.D.

It's hard for me to comprehend

There ever was 383 ...

With New World restlessness in me.

I wonder what it means to live

Amidst a timelessness like this... .

I do not like my rootlessness,

At least not so today.

I want to feel my roots run deep,

And have within the simple sense

Of who I am, from whence I've come

And where I'll finally rest in sleep.

As I read these lines written so many years ago, I wonder: What does it mean to have "my roots run deep"? Living in the same village, believing what my ancient ancestors believed? Or does it mean finding spiritual roots within that awaken a new discovery of "who I am"?

There's the essential tension in life: How can I break free from a robotic belief in whatever I learned as a little one and, while I discover my own unique essence, still honor that tradition? How can I get "unstuck" from ego narrowness, find my essence, and stay connected?

If one is to get unstuck, understanding the following is critical! When we are born, our Essence is uniquely present. We have our own differing temperaments and a capability for full emotional expression. We cry; we are angry, sad, frustrated, joyful, afraid, tranquil, excited, and pleased; and our mood switches quickly.

We have no language, so we experience the world tactilely, firsthand one might say, as our fingers and mouth endlessly touch and taste whatever is available. If we're fortunate enough to be born with all our senses, we see purely and hear without judgment. Our perception is clean, that is, without judgments and prejudices. Let circle A in Figure 1 represent this child, or Real-Self, state.

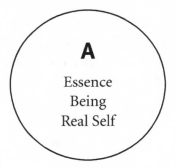

Figure 1: Child State

The task of parents is to prepare the baby for life as the parents know it. A certain language is spoken. The young child is taught *not* to say and do certain things. "Don't tell Aunt Susie that she's ugly!" "Don't take off your clothes in public!" Confusing instructions about emotionality are given: "Don't be angry!" or "Don't feel sad!" We are rarely told that feelings *just are* and are okay, and it's how you express them that matters. These are the lessons of ego development.

Conditions are imposed (of course) on the child's behavior. The child learns to associate "self-worth" with these conditions. "Mommy/Daddy won't/will love you if…" The child learns acceptable ways to quarrel in their particular family and unacceptable ways. One may be taught (through observation of parents and siblings) to walk away from conflict, another to stay and win, another to compromise and negotiate, another to give in to avoid something worse. The child is taught loyalty to family, religion, country and even passionate loyalty to the local or national soccer or football team.[6] This sets up a deep conflict between the essence, or Real-Self, which one continues to experience viscerally and the emerging conditioned second hand learning Ego-self.

These are important learnings. Teaching these things is the job of parents and the family. They are, however, simply what we learn and are not our essence. They are secondhand learning (our ego), and this is illustrated by the fact that the baby born in Italy and the one in China or even the one born to the family next door learns significantly different things. Let those secondhand learnings be illustrated by circle B in Figure 2:

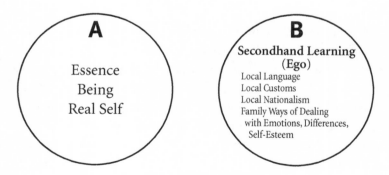

Figure 2: Ego Development

The process of "growing up" means that A is nearly swallowed up by B (Figure 3).

---

6   All of my children (now ages 40–50) are somewhat brainwashed Pittsburgh Steeler and Pirate fans.

Figure 3: Real Self Obscured by Ego

By the teen years, one's essence (A) is almost completely obscured. Even physiological capabilities are influenced. Humans are born crying. By the teen years the ability to cry has been seriously impaired, especially in males.

"Psychologists estimate that by the end of early childhood the average person has had twenty-five thousand hours of ... programming from parents or whomever is doing the child rearing. (Plenty of these) were never anything more than the reflective behaviors of care-givers stumbling along"[7] (and intending their best.)

Emotional development has been enriched or thwarted by this time and is carried into adult life. Touch is viewed differently. In many cultures, as in Italy, I can easily greet a man with a kiss on both cheeks. Not so in America.

The obscuring of one's essence is further evidenced in the teen years by conformity in dress styles and in "what's hip" and what isn't. Teens live in conformity with their parents' expectations, or are in reaction to them and live in conformance with peers and the influence of the media.

Such secondhand learnings prepare us to live as (hopefully) decent citizens in our culture. They are crucial to our development. *But they are not who we are!*

---

7   Scherer, John. Work and the Human Spirit. p.122.

Unless one addresses the shrinking of the essence (A), one will go through life primarily wearing masks that reflect second-hand learnings. I may live my entire life thinking that this is who I am: I am my clothes. I am my job. I am my bank account. I am my political, social and religious beliefs.

Therefore I never really live—never experience my own true being—my Real-Self—my essence!

> I do not know the man so bold
>
> He dare in lonely place
>
> That awful stranger Consciousness
>
> Deliberately face.
>
> —*Emily Dickinson*

As I become more conscious, more aware of my inner voice, I recognize that my secondhand learnings—my ego—are a "pretend self" fashioned for me with love by my parents to ensure my survival. I have learned these lessons unconsciously and, thanks to them, can move through life with reasonable success. My ego-self navigates the world pretty well.

But the one thing that's true of my ego-self is that it is dreadfully fragile and requires regular defensive action to protect it. For example, if my ego-self is my opinions, watch out if your views differ from mine! I am thus called to defend my ego again and again. All defense is defense of ego.

On the other hand, essence needs no defense. I will defend and explain—at the drop of a hat—my religion, my country's decisions, my way of handling this and that conflict or difference. I do all this without knowing that those things I am defending aren't me—my essential Real-Self—but are the result of my secondhand learnings.

The conditioning of our minds (secondhand learning) as a German, Russian, American or Chinese, blinds us to the dark side of our own country and makes us susceptible to false rumors. For instance, for three years after 9/11, roughly half of all Americans continued to believe that there were Iraqis in the planes that brought down the World Trade Center on 9/11. (There were none.)

So, while my ego may provide me with certain survival advantages, it can also so blind me that I am unable to differentiate between factual information and my nationalistic secondhand learning: illustrated with the phrase "My country, right or wrong."

The journey of Life is both the process and the goal of expanding my awareness of my shrunken essence, observing the secondhand learning which obscures it, and freeing myself—my Real-Self—as in Figure 4.

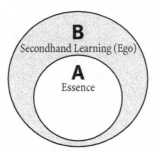

Figure 4: The Triumph of Essence

When people confuse Ego-Self with Real-Self (being), their life becomes complicated. So, the first step in simplicity is to unravel these two selves.

There will always be ego. I will be proud—that's ego. I will be embarrassed—that's ego. As a mature, spiritual being I observe my ego, rein it in sometimes—and sometimes not. One must recover that essence with which we were born to find peace in life, to acknowledge that we couldn't have managed without our secondhand learning, and to know again our child essence, curiosity, and awe in a new, adult way.

> We shall not cease from exploration
>
> And the end of that exploring
>
> Will be to arrive at where we started
>
> And know that place for the first time!
>
> —*T.S. Elliot*

Jesus is quoted (in Luke 18:17), "Whoever does not receive the kingdom of God like a little child will never enter it." This kingdom, he says elsewhere, is "within"! (Luke 17:21)[8] Now certainly he doesn't mean to become childish. Rather, he asks us to find that child again and, as an adult, give ourselves freedom to wander and wonder; to open wide the window of our life, so that fresh breezes, from far beyond our secondhand learning, can enter.

That's the journey.

We can honor our ethnic god and ethnic customs. That history helped make sense out of life for our ancestors. We are not, however, our ethnicity. You and I are far more than that in our being. We must see through our language, customs, religion, and nation to our essence. These are important, but don't get stuck there! Let them become transparent! Then you can see through them to the mystery beyond that is indescribable and unknown—your source, our source, one source. The profound mystery of Life.

And most important:

Relax.

The mystery remains.

Give yourself peace.

---

8 My friend, and in this case, critic friend—Dr. James B. Recob writes, "While this may illustrate his point, his truncated quotation does violence to Jesus' meaning. Luke tells us that Jesus said to the quarrelsome Pharisees who had asked when the Kingdom of God would come, "The Kingdom of God is within YOU (plural)" — this might also be translated "the Kingdom of God is among you" or "in your midst" (which might even mean that the kingdom is already here!). Far from being a distinctly individualistic, interior entity, the Kingdom is social, its location is in the corporate body of humankind—including even the Pharisees! In any event, the plural YOU at the end of this quotation rules out a purely individualistic understanding of Jesus' spirituality."

Est—This is it!

Tat Tvam Asi

You are that mystery, and it is more than you. Give yourself this peace that passeth understanding—the wisdom of not knowing. As in the final scene of "2001 Space Odyssey," when the astronaut has left the mother ship and is hurtling into the unknown, "We are in a free fall into a future that is mysterious."[9] We should just embrace the wonder, choosing not to waste our energy in a futile attempt to stop the fall or to define the future.

---

9   Joseph Campbell.

CHAPTER THREE: ON A CLEAR DAY

*T*oday, once again it is a "bellissima giornata"—a beautiful day. Our hosts, Enrico and Rita, take us in their SUV into the mountains of the Chianti region where the freshness of the air, the scents of lavender and pine, and the touch of chestnut leaves blend in a rich, earthy paradise for the senses. Chianti's well-balanced ecology is a sight to behold—to smell, to taste, to hear, to touch—and the day is so clear that it seems we can see all the way to forever.

However, for me, clear and bright as this day was, a "bellissima giornata" is not about the weather outside.

> On a clear day
>
> Rise and look around you
>
> And you'll see who you are.
>
> On a clear day
>
> How it will astound you
>
> That the glow of your being
>
> Outshines every star!
>
> You feel part of every mountain, sea, and
> shore.
>
> You can hear from far and near
>
> A sound you've never heard before.
>
> On a clear day
>
> On that clear day
>
> You can see forever and ever more.[10]

---

[10] Lyrics by Alan Jay Lerner for the Broadway musical, "On a Clear Day You Can See Forever," 1965.

As you read these lyrics, did you take them literally? Are you someone who, if you heard me singing these words on a rainy day in Seattle, might say that the song wasn't suitable at that moment?

That's a very common response. And if it is yours, I suggest that you have discovered some unconscious literalism in yourself. Surely, you don't believe, upon conscious reflection, that the song-writer was actually claiming that you can't know "who you are" when it isn't literally clear and sunny outside.

These lyrics illustrate both the reality of literalness and the reality of deeper meaning—of metaphor, of mythic proportions. The lyrics also highlight how easy it is to only see—or as one might also say, "to get hooked into"—the literal. And to be perfectly *clear* about it, let me say that this song is about the Internal Self seeing clearly!

The fifth chakra[11] in Hinduism is about clarity. Without clarity there is no possibility of mature spiritual growth. William Blake, the 19th century English poet, artist and spiritual guide put it this way: "When the doors of perception are cleansed, everything appears as it actually is, infinite."

Whew! Okay. I see through my eyes, —but do I see what's out there, or are my perceptions so clouded that I merely project (like a movie projector on a screen) what's inside me from my ego development? What clouds my perception? Let's find out.

Take part in an activity with me. Look at someone else and only after you describe what you *see* and *hear*, continue reading.

> Did you see someone …
>
> … being silly or
>
> …acting foolish or

---

11 The lower three chakras (between the anus and the genitals of the element Earth; the genitals of the element Water; and the navel of the element Fire).are about surviving, reproduction and power. These humans share with animals. The fourth chakra (heart) is compassion, of the element Air, which transforms the lower chakras from reactivity (like a reptile) to conscious creating. At Chakra four we are, "freed from the dictatorship of the species," as Joseph Campbell says. Simply put, reproduction and power are now transformed to a loving function. The fifth chakra (throat) furthers the spiritual and uniquely human capability through clarity.

...making fun of you or

...being friendly or

...thinking you're ridiculous or

...looking kindly or

...feeling nervous?

If so, you are describing not what you see but what you think! And your perception is *clouded!*

The above statements are not descriptions but, rather, are judgments or thoughts that come from within you and tell about your unique ego way of perceiving certain others (based, by the way, on what you learned in the first ten or so years of your life).

That's fine! Your thoughts and judgments are fine for you to notice and to acknowledge to yourself. They are the prejudices or *pre-judgments* that you lay on others. Know this about yourself and do not confuse your internal judgments and projections with what is observable "out there." These projections are inside you and describe your "in here," not the "out there."

Statements like:

He is selfish.

She is controlling.

They hate our values.

They don't care about others.

He is overbearing.

She thinks she is better than others.

are projections. That is, they tell about your *judgments* when you see certain behaviors. They are what you are *thinking,* not what you are *seeing!* They are your ego-truth but not THE truth. When you think/speak this way, you are *clouded.*

When you say these things to others, you are stating *your* truth but *not* THE truth about what's "out there"; rather you are stating the truth about your ego lens. Being unclear, themselves, about these distinctions, they will likely take your projections personally and then defend themselves and strike back in some way. This is *not* straight talk. This creates and inflames conflict or differences.

Try again. Look at someone and only after you describe what you *see* and *hear*, continue reading.

If you said (assuming accuracy here), "I see blue eyes blinking occasionally, the head slightly tilted, the mouth suddenly opening as I hear 'Ha-ha!' and now the head moving from left to right and back," you are beginning to see clearly!

You also have thoughts. For every thought there is an emotion. For instance, if your thought is that "He is selfish," is your emotional state (that is, your feeling) likely to be one of these: frustrated, angry, unhappy, disdainful, sad, fearful? Or one of these: pleased, trusting, warm?

Of course, it is the former. Clarity about what you sense (see, hear, touch, smell, taste) must be separate from what you think (your judgments and interpretations), from your emotions, from your wants—and finally, from your choice of words or actions.

Otherwise, you will think your projections are the "truth" about another person and what's "out there." Also, you may be prone to believe stories someone tells you about another person as the literal truth, rather than as their projections or, at least, as their *interpretation* of what was said. When someone says to you, "Jane said this about you," are you likely to believe the gossip literally, or to hold it in your mind as this person's unique story—but not necessarily what *Jane* said or meant? If you accept the story as the truth then you are being a literalist.

This is not about the integrity of the person telling you the story. Humans don't remember accurately, since words are filtered through lack of attentiveness, bias, interpretations unique to the receiver and the ever-active emotional field. If it was more than "hi" or "thanks," try to remember the exact words you've said and heard in the last 30 minutes. Humans remember the meaning they derived or the meaning they intended but they do not—especially if emotionality escalates—remember the exact words.

It is this simple! You have an intention; you express it through face, eyes, tone, posture and perhaps, words. The other interprets all these (especially the first four!) and derives a meaning. The meaning they take determines their emotionality in that second. If it is not the meaning you intended, then we have what John Wallen calls the "Interpersonal Gap"[12]—that is, there is a misunderstanding, which is, in life, the major source of relational conflict! If either of you is behaving "literalistically," then you will be *sure* that your interpretation is right or the truth, and that there is no misunderstanding or reason to work it through and find out the original intent. Such a literalist will also be sure they know "exactly what was said," will blame you for "making them feel" whatever they now feel—based not, of course, on your actions or what you said, but on their very unique personal *interpretation* of what you said and did.

But at that literalistic moment, *they don't get it!* They may even unknowingly say, "I know you by your actions," (Rather than how they uniquely interpreted your actions!) Worse, if you try to unravel the misunderstanding by paraphrasing (which is to check with the other about whether the meaning you took from her actions and words was what she intended) the literalist will resist, since she already is *sure* it is not a misunderstanding.

These are critical distinctions to make in life if one is to get "unstuck" from one's childhood beliefs and engage others in dialogue rather than argument.

We create our own emotions because we create our own interpretations and judgments. Nobody "makes" us feel. If you think so, you are living a reactive life, and you are not your own Self. You have not risen above the three animal chakras.

---

[12] For where to read more about the Interpersonal Gap see the selected bibliography: Wallen, John

If you think we should "do what we feel," then you are proclaiming a reactive philosophy. Don't "do what you feel." Instead, "feel what you feel" and "choose what you do." Do not be a slave to feelings which come from your judgments and beliefs that are secondhand learning. See clearly, transcending the prejudices of many around you.

Get unstuck.

Chapter Four: Distinctions
Freedom, God, Faith, Doubt and The Force

"Well, okay," you say. "I like all this freedom. But how does freedom interface with boundaries, with structure?"

A question you probably didn't ask.

Please do.

Ah, thank you.

John Dewey, the philosopher said something like, "There is no freedom without structure." Paul Cezanne, the French artist, attempted to find a balance between "impressions" and structure. Prior to photography, artists attempted to accurately reproduce scenes. This was called "Realism."

After photography, some artists (called Impressionists) began to paint their impressions (perceptions) of landscape and humans. That is, they began to paint, not what a camera could reproduce, but their own unique impression of that which they were seeing. Monet painted his unique impression of a sunrise from which the word "Impressionists" arose.

Cezanne was influenced by that movement, but wanted more. He searched for structure within the freedom of Impressionism. This is called *post*-Impressionism and became a strong influence on the next phase of art, brilliantly manifested by Picasso.

So what? When we break away from secondhand learning— or better yet—when we go beyond or through, without disrespecting, secondhand learning, we experience freedom and a new internal structure. We have shed the "should" and "should-not" shackles and found our own internal guide. The eternal dragon with scales reading "Thou Shalt" and "Thou Shalt Not" is still within sight, but has been subdued by the genuine "you" within—that inner voice.

St. Augustine said, "Love God and do as you please!" The assumption here is that if you love Self and God (or whatever you call the indescribable ultimate energy or source), then you will please to do that which connects you to all Creation! The fear is that, without a heavy-handed authoritarian structure, people will run amok. Responding to that fear, Robert Sapolsky of Stanford University writes that "... it's obvious that there's no shortage of folks running amok [already] thanks to their belief."

> External, secondhand "shoulds" need no
>   longer control your life.

> This is true freedom.

> This is true structure.

In addition, there's something truly freeing about challenging our secondhand beliefs: We have the freedom to actually experience things differently from one another.

One night (August 29, 2004), Patricia and I had a profound experience in Verona's 2000-year-old Roman Coliseum as the opera *Aida* was performed. Even though we were together, side-by-side, focusing on the same scene as it unfolded, we each had our own unique personal experience. As we shared our experiences, each of us was amazed by what we missed that the other saw or heard or otherwise "experienced."

We left saying that this experience was both individual and indescribable. Wanting nevertheless to capture my evening for posterity, I imagined myself playing the music to someone back home. I looked for a video of the performance. But, while I will still try to find one, I realize that, for both Patricia and myself, the evening was one of those many profound events in life that are ... well, simply indescribable. There are no words for it. One reason for this is that words have already-assigned (one could say "secondhand") meanings. This works out fine, usually: When we say, "It's snowing," others know what we mean. However, Eskimos have twenty-some words for "snow" to depict all the various kinds that they experience. When we say "God," in whatever language, we are generally talking about a "supreme Creator." But the word points to many different experiences.

"God" is an English word that means the same as "Deo" (Latin), "Allah" (Arabic), or the word Jesus used—"Allaha" (Aramaic). Every language has its word for "God." And these words mean something different, not only to the various religions (and the hundreds or thousands of different divisions within those religions) but to the individual adherents of the same "division" or "expression."

More importantly, the word itself points *to* something beyond itself. The word "God" is our feeble attempt to define or name that which cannot be defined or named—the primal source of all life energy. That primal source is indescribable, and the moment we try to define it, we not only narrow that which is indescribable but we also create divisions with those who describe it differently.

Patricia and I did not argue about whose experience was the "right" one, nor did we parse the language we used to describe the evening to each other. We simply found delight in the way we each could expand, from our own experience, the experience of the other. But language would always fall short, since the essential experience each of us had was indescribable. Or, as the theologians might say, "ineffable." Mysterious.

How much more so is the primal life-source! And saying "God" is a first attempt to describe the mystery. But, paradoxically, this English masculine word, like all its synonyms in English and other languages, immediately limits one's ability to communicate an experience of the indescribable. Thus, this whatever-ness remains a mystery. And we may simply have no choice but to leap into it, to have faith in "the substance of things hoped for, the evidence of things not seen."[13]

Faith and doubt are twins. I once heard Howard Thurman[14] say:

"I take the leap of faith and I discover within myself a new, fresh affirmation! I celebrate. And then always within me there is the rumor that I may be wrong! That's my growing edge!"

"Doubt is not the opposite of faith; it is one element of faith," wrote Paul Tillich. Faith without doubt is a dead, secondhand faith. Faith with doubt is dynamic, pointing us to further growth and understanding. Elsewhere, Thurman wrote: "There is something in every one of you that waits and listens for the sound of the genuine in yourself. It is the only true guide you will ever have. And if you cannot hear it, you will all of your life spend your days on the ends of strings that somebody else pulls."

Literalists about doctrine or about their own scriptures live on the ends of strings that somebody else pulls. Tony Van Renterghem[14] describes the difference this way:

> For thousands of years, man's approach to religion has been a conflict between two concepts:

> The Celebrant: The individual who personally tried to understand the meaning of life by loving and living it to the hilt, who watched the infinity of the star-studded skies, rejoiced about the daily return of the sun, celebrated the excitement of the hunt, the ecstasy of sex, and the miracle of birth, all the while feeling that he

---

[13] Hebrews 11:1.

[14] In 1953-54, I was blessed with the opportunity to hear Howard Thurman, Dean of the Chapel at Boston University, each Sunday evening sharing more about his morning sermon. He had been a fellow student of Martin Luther King's father and was a mentor for Martin, Jr., who was a student at Boston University and who (apparently) attended these same Sunday evening sessions. In Ursula King's book *Christian Mystics* Thurman is described as a 20th century mystic along with such notables as Thomas Merton, Pierre Teilhard de Chardin, Simone Weil, and the Dalai Lama.

[14] This is from Van Renterghem's book *When Santa Was a Shaman*. See the Selected Bibliography for more information.

himself was part of the Life Force, which would joyfully reclaim him at the end of his days.

The Worshiper: One whose faith was based on fear and awe of a Force of infinite power and authority, a jealous god who had to be flattered, worshiped, appeased, and bargained with in the same manner that one had to deal with the old chief of the clan. Hence, one made deals with him to obtain favours, to be "saved," or to be forgiven for one's feelings of guilt for cultural or ritual trespasses (sin). But how could one make such deals? Well, as with the chief, by dealing with those who let it be known that only they knew the word of God and how to get through to him (often at a price).

The conflict between these two concepts still bedevils our present-day religions, with the fundamentalists as the standard-bearers of "Worship." Most religions, however, seem to contain elements of both concepts.

Religions commonly arise out of culture and environment; they spread with the culture, and are usually forced upon conquered populations. Even if the new culture becomes popular and the new religion takes hold, undercurrents of the old culture and religion continue to exist and tend to resurface as soon as the new power structure and its religion show signs of weakening.

Our customs and religions are imprinted on our minds: they are absorbed uncritically beginning in early childhood, and are further imprinted throughout the rest of our lives. Consequently, we rarely have a critical understanding of our own religion and its social, cultural, political, and economic effects. History shows that our position toward other religious points of view is only tolerant when their social, political, and economic aims coincide with those of our own culture. When aims conflict—as they did during the Inquisition and the Holocaust, as well as today in Northern Ireland, India, the Balkans, and the Middle East—religion will break its most basic precepts of peace and love to lash out murderously.

Clarity about "the worshiper" or what I identify with Christian Literalism or Fundamentalism is critical if one is to break free and become a "celebrant of life" who finds one's authority from within as one experiences a unity with a "Life Force." *May you realize the force that is within you!*

30

PART TWO: CHRISTIAN FUNDAMENTALISM:
A Distraction From Essence

Along the road to Volpaia.

CHAPTER FIVE:
WHAT IS CHRISTIAN LITERALISM?

*D*uring these sun-filled weeks in Italy, I have talked to many Europeans, including, certainly, Italians, about the so-called "Christian Right" in the U.S. They just don't get it. It is not in their experience. Biblical literalism hardly exists there— although blind allegiance to church doctrines or literal beliefs about saints or relics certainly exists!

Many pagan (peasant) religious symbols can still be found in Christian churches in Italy. Italy is a secular country, if measured by its low birth rates, openness to free expression, legal abortion, low church attendance, and the crisis of a declining number of priests. Catholics are rarely Biblical literalists. They adhere to Catholic teaching (some only when convenient), which is held above Biblical authority in Catholic faith.

In this country of *la dolce vita* (the sweet life), I am on my journey, in both Tuscany and Life, to make sense of it all. And it seems useful to begin at the beginning which, for me, means to look at definitions.

Words like "liberal," "conservative," and "fundamentalist" get bandied about as if they meant the same thing to each person. They are often used in a pejorative way, as if it is bad or ignorant to be so labeled. But to have any kind of reasonable discussion about the different viewpoints each word represents, it is useful to set out some generally accepted definitions that I've culled from the Oxford Dictionary:

Liberal: One who

    … is open-minded.

    … is not strict or rigorous, nor literal in making
       interpretations.

... favors individual liberty and political and
social reform.

... regards many traditional beliefs as dispensable,
invalidated by modern thought or liable to
change.

Conservative: One who

... tends to conserve.

... is adverse to rapid change.

... is moderate and avoids extremes.

...allows only minor changes in traditional
ritual, etc.

Fundamentalist: One who

... strictly maintains traditional protestant beliefs
such as the inerrancy of Scripture and literal
acceptance of the creeds.

... strictly maintains ancient and fundamental
doctrines of any religion.

I would add that fundamentalists regard such beliefs as
absolute and give them supremacy over civil proclamations.

Missing in the Oxford Dictionary definition of liberal is the
distinction between liberal as a process (i.e., openness) and liberal
as ideas or beliefs held (i.e., pro-choice or pro-civil rights). Liberal
beliefs can be held just as dogmatically as conservative or fundamentalist ideas.

My parents were what by these definitions would be called
"conservative."[16] They were born into Christian families who had
accepted their heritage for 15 centuries as Christians in Europe and

---

[16] John Green distinguishes between Evangelical (Southern Baptists, Assemblies of
God, Missouri Synod Lutherans, many smaller denominations, and non-denominational) and mainline Protestants (Methodists, Presbyterians, Episcopalians,
Lutherans and others). He lists sub-categories in each of these (and Catholic) as
Traditionalists, Centrists and Modernists. Christian Literalism is almost synony-
mous with Traditionalism which is the position of half the Evangelicals but a very
small percentage of mainline Protestants and Catholics.

America. I suspect that my dad's Christian lineage goes back to when our Druid ancestors were converted by a Roman sword.

They baptized their children, prayed daily, said grace before meals, worked hard, read the Bible, went to church every Sunday (morning and evening), taught Sunday School, joined the Ku Klux Klan (as noted in the afterward) when the beloved preacher who baptized me and my mother's saintly father said they should, and tithed (gave one tenth of their income to the church) even during the Depression, when money was scarce.

Because they trusted their preacher, my parents, quite naively, joined the Klan, not realizing what kind of extremist group it was. For them, it was like joining a socially-oriented religious club. It was a values choice, not driven by overt malice towards Catholics, Jews and Blacks.

The Klan (originally birthed in Indiana) spread rapidly in the North (Indiana, Ohio, Pennsylvania, and New York states) in the 1920s and, at least for my parents, also died quickly. They knew nothing about the extremely dark side of the Klan or the acts of violence until years later, when they were extremely embarrassed by their former association with it and renounced it. I was in eighth grade when my teacher talked negatively about the Klan. My mother met my teacher the next day to explain that the Klan was a fine Christian group. Since she had sworn to keep its secrets, she was hesitant to let me read the little brown Klan book when we returned home after meeting with my teacher. But she did so, and soon I confronted her in the kitchen.

"Mother, have you read this?" I asked.

"No, but I knew it was okay because my father and our preacher said so," she replied.

"Well, mother, listen to this." I then read the part about protecting the chastity of white women. She was shocked as I read on. Almost immediately, my parents did a 180-degree turn in their thinking. I'm proud of that, and I'm forever grateful that they were open to change and were willing to be influenced by their 14-year-old son. Embarrassed, they then asked me to keep their former membership a secret! But what has stayed with me all these years is the example they set of a willingness to examine their beliefs and behavior, take into account new information, search for consistency and continuity, and make changes as a result.

Thus, while their orientation in matters of religion and politics was certainly conservative, my parents were willing to set aside absolutist dogma when it didn't match with their developing spiritual insights. And in later years, their strong stand for civil rights, heartfelt hospitality towards my African-American, Catholic and Jewish friends, ecumenical Bible study with Catholics in the early 1960's, and their acceptance of the pacifist position towards war (Dad was a World War I veteran) evidenced their openness.

This family history has helped me to understand (though not at all agree with) conservative Christians in various countries—including ours today, who, it seems, automatically fall in line with their governments in times of war. It seems that nationalism, for conservatives, often trumps their faith. A favorite verse quoted to support this is, "Obey them that have the rule over you and submit yourselves." (Hebrews 13:17, Titus 3:1, I Peter 2:13). There are notable exceptions to this stance, such as the Amish, Mennonites, Quakers, Jehovah's Witnesses and a few other small denominations.

Millions of decent, ordinary, German citizens supported Hitler and his anti-gay, anti-Jewish values[17] (some others, such as Lutheran pastors Dietrich Bonhoeffer and Martin Niemoller chose imprisonment and death). Most of the German soldiers fighting us in World War II were Christians. Russian Orthodox Christians, suppressed as they were and therefore perhaps wisely so, supported their state. In the Balkans in the 1990's, the Roman Catholics of

---

[17] The loss of six million Jews in death camps is widely known. That 500,000 (assumed) gays were killed is less known. (Also gypsies suffered deeply).

Croatia, the Muslims of Bosnia-Herzegovina, and the Orthodox Christians of Serbia mostly supported their government against the others.[18] It is easy for us to "demonize" those who commit atrocities as if we – you and me – might not turn our eye away or even do the same. How many Americans protested the internment of American citizens of Japanese descent in World War II? My family didn't, and I didn't.

The major U.S. support for the American war in Iraq comes from conservatives and, especially, fundamentalists.

There is a thin line that divides those ordinary people who joined the Klan from those who did violence carrying the Klan cross. A thin line between those ordinary people who staffed Hitler's camps and those who stayed silent. A thin line between those Americans who torture and abuse detainees while denying them their legal and human rights and those of us who turn our eye away. Do not cast stones. Each of us is responsible for injustice anywhere because each is everyone and the mask of indifference and the mask of bigotry hovers above, ready to slip down on us at any unaware moment.

Perhaps it is about different ways of holding beliefs.

A black and white, what we might call "absolutist," point of view is more apt to be a position of fundamentalist Christians than conservative or more liberal Christians who tend to be more nuanced. Certainly though, there is a liberal extreme, its own kind of "true belief" constituency that can cross that thin line.

But my main focus, here, is to demonstrate the political tendency of American Christian Fundamentalism (Traditionalism in Greene's definition). That tendency is towards theocracy[19] rather than democracy, and towards nationalism rather than internationalism. That is, the fundamentalist agenda would take certain personal beliefs and make them the law of the land. Abortion, stem-cell

---

[18] The situation of the moderate inclusive Muslims in this war must not be equated with the strident, aggressive Christian Serbia and (perhaps less so) Christian Croatia.

[19] Theocracy: Government of a state by assumed divine guidance.

research, gay rights, school prayer, and the use of the word God or other religious matters like the display of the Ten Commandments are examples of this. This is *not* wrong. But it is different from the sharp church/state separation that (most) conservatives and liberals want imposed.

Over 200 years ago, many of our founding fathers were Unitarian[20] (not Trinitarian[21]). When someone suggested prayer at the constitutional convention, it was decisively voted down. They had fled from a theocratic Europe and insisted on a strict separation of church and state.

My parents remained conservative in their beliefs all of their lives. My father was curious about and would read "liberal" scholars' books. He deeply appreciated and studied Goodspeed's *Life of Jesus* and his *Paul* and was intrigued by the idea (put forth in 1850 by Renan) that Jesus was born in Nazareth, not Bethlehem.

Fundamentalism was very influential as a political force in the early 1950s. Seeing the world in black and white terms, certain fundamentalists were behind the listing by Senator McCarthy and Congressman Velde of liberal and even conservative citizens as "Communists." Members of the Methodist Youth groups (Epworth League) were so listed. Anyone who supported US-Soviet relations during World War II (the Soviets were our allies against Hitler!) could expect to be listed as a Communist sympathizer. Bishop G. Bromley Oxnam of the Methodist Church was attacked publicly again and again by the House Un-American Activities Committee (HUAC), which was led by Congressman Velde from Illinois, as being a Communist. When Bishop Oxnam appeared before HUAC, he carefully dissected their accusations. He produced a letter dated November, 1945 from the then General Dwight D. Eisenhower (the U.S. President at the time of these hearings) wishing Oxnam the "utmost success in the worthy work" of American-Soviet friendship.

---

[20] Oneness of Deity.

[21] God the father, Son, and Holy Spirit (Three as One)

When Bishop Oxnam faced HUAC, he was without any information from the committee about the substance of its accusations. But he guessed correctly that the source was a fundamentalist Christian group that called themselves the American Council of Churches.[22] Their president was The Reverend W.O.H. Garman who, along with two colleagues, reserved front row seats at the Bishop's hearings. Bishop Oxnam was relieved when he saw them walk into this crowded hearing to their special seats. He knew he had guessed correctly about the source of the damaging allegations. After that hearing, HUAC lost its influence.

Dad had face-to-face contact with McCarthyism when a church trustee brought the McCarthy-Velde nightmare to our neighborhood. As it happened, The Reverend Garman was also pastor of a church just six blocks from my parents' home and from their church, the United Brethren Church in Wilkinsburg, Pennsylvania, where my dad was the Superintendent of the Sunday school. My Sunday school teacher supported Reverend Garman and was a very influential member and trustee of our church. He bought fundamentalist literature, alleging that our church and our pastor had Communist leanings, and attempted to distribute it to the congregation.

The result was a face-off between my eighth-grade educated dad (railroad worker, Steel Worker's Union member) and this wealthy trustee of the church. My father simply picked up the several boxes of books and threw them in the church furnace!

It may seem otherwise, but my dad was actually a very gentle man. In this case he simply held the "conservative" line supporting the curriculum of the United Brethren Church against those who wanted, in addition to adding the books mentioned above, to substitute the church curriculum with literature from a fundamentalist "non-denominational" publisher. What my father did here was to *preserve* and *conserve* what he regarded as the doctrine of his

---

22 This "American" Council of Churches should not be confused with the mainline Protestant/Orthodox National Council of Churches headquartered in New York City.

religion against interlopers. But he never suggested that his beliefs were the only *true* beliefs.

Yes, I'm proud of my dad. Yes, of course, this story is through the lens of a son who cherishes these stories. One year, there stood at the altar ("communion rail") 22 new members of this conservative mainline Protestant United Brethren Church. All 22 had been visited by my dad. The pastor often acknowledged dad's role and influence with these 22 and in the larger life of the church.

These experiences illustrate my definition of "conservatism." But how am I using the word "fundamentalism"? First, a disclaimer: I will not define fundamentalism as it applies to other faiths except to say that it implies a belief that the adherents of that faith or, more likely, that branch of the faith, are following the one and only true revelation. Thus, even others of the same religion are infidels or non-believers.

Now, some history: In Protestant Christianity, a series of watershed conferences were held in Niagara, New York, from 1883 to 1897. At these Bible conferences, conservative Christians gathered in reaction to what they labeled "modernism" and "liberalism"—to establish the principles of Christian Fundamentalism. Fundamentalism, worldwide, is a reaction to the modernization (secularism) of culture which is why Muslim militant fundamentalism is a late 20th century phenomenon. It is also a response to oppressive authoritarian governments in the middle east. Almost without exception the U.S. has supported these governments (including Saddam Hussein until about 1990.) Sayyid Qutb was the real founder of modern Islamic fundamentalism. He was executed by al-Nasser (Egypt) in 1966. Thus, Protestant fundamentalism pre-dates Islamic by 50-60 years.

In 1898, Albert Schweitzer, the world-famous missionary to Africa, published his *The Quest for the Historical Jesus*, which, as I say elsewhere in this book, shocked the conservative world. Perhaps "shocked" is too strong a word. After all, the German scholars had been applying literary methods to the study of Biblical documents (i.e., how did the Bible *really* develop?) since 1850. Centuries earlier, various scholars had challenged traditional beliefs about Biblical authorship. The Frenchman, Renan, wrote his *Life of Jesus*, including the words, "Jesus was born at Nazareth" (not Bethlehem). Countless other scholars and archaeologists were enthusiastically pursuing such knowledge about the origins of the Old and New Testaments. Such teaching was being presented in mainline Protestant seminaries and starting to be reflected in sermons by the more educated (and courageous) ministers.

In 1910, the General Assembly of the Presbyterian Church distilled what was agreed on at the Niagara Bible Conferences into five fundamentals:

1. The *Inerrancy* of Scriptures. There are no errors or contradictions.

2. The *Literal* Virgin Birth of Jesus by Mary without human intercourse.

3. The *Blood* (Substitutionary) Atonement. Jesus' death was like the Old Testament sacrifices of lambs. Jesus shed blood to save us. This was God's intention and plan.

4. *Physical* Bodily Resurrection of Jesus Christ. This was not only a spiritual or "soul" event but, rather, his whole body was raised.

5. *Bodily* Second Coming of Jesus. Jesus, in the body, will come again—not simply in a spiritual return. He will be visible and initiate the end of history.

If you don't believe these "fundamentals," you are not a Christian! It's that simple in their belief.

At ages 15-17, I was influenced by the "Youth for Christ" fundamentalist movement. Rather suddenly, I was preaching to my conservative pastor and to other pastors in our district. The churches of our conservative church, The United Brethren in Christ, were organized geographically. As Youth President of the District, I invited Dave Nettleton of Youth for Christ to preach at a district rally on the subject "You Must Be Born Again." How's that for both being very committed to the fundamentalist version of Christianity and displaying the arrogance of a 16-year-old trying to "bring the truth" to the very pastors who had nourished me but whom I now viewed as "not saved" as evidenced by their lack of emphasis on preaching the five fundamentals!

Then I went to one of our church colleges (Otterbein in Westerville, Ohio). There I met compassionate and intellectual professors. My fundamentalism began to unravel as I studied the history of the Christian church and the long, slow development of what Christians call "the scriptures" and from the influences of a liberal arts environment of literature, philosophy, sociology, psychology and so forth.

This period of rediscovery was accelerated at the United Theological Seminary in Dayton, Ohio. I began to see fundamentalist Christianity as a belief system rather than faith—that is, it was about their "right beliefs", especially the inerrancy of the Bible. It guarantees "certainty." It provides the definitive answers with a selectivist approach that emphasizes certain scriptural verses and ignores others (i.e. "an eye for an eye" versus "Love your enemy…If someone strikes you on one cheek turn to him your other also.") If you don't accept any one of the five fundamentals or the so-called "moral" positions, then you are not a Christian! It's not even about being "saved" or "born again", which are favorite conservative phrases. You must both be saved and believe the "right" beliefs. There is no unknowing, no mystery and therefore no need for faith.

Protestant fundamentalism has also had a social agenda (as do liberal and conservative movements). Currently, that social agenda is dominated by issues of abortion, embryonic cell research, gay marriage, school prayer,[23] and increasingly how not to obstruct the Second Coming of Jesus—when, of course, those who believe the fundamentals and are saved will be happily separated from the rest of us who, along with this author, will burn. The success (over 60 million copies sold) of the *Left Behind* series, and the latest in that series, *Glorious Appearing*, which details the fate of non-believers, is testimony to the growing American fundamentalist movement of roughly 40 million adult adherents.

It is because this movement is strongly allied with the Bush administration, with its finger on our military trigger, that polls have consistently indicated that most of the world (certainly in Europe, the Mid-East, and even our Australian allies[24],) fears American Fundamentalism as much as Islamic Fundamentalism. The word "crusade" mentioned just once (unintentionally, I believe) by the President and anti-Muslim statements by supporters fuel that fear. The degree to which the President holds fundamentalist views about the "last days" (the Apocalypse) and the Israel-Palestinian and wider, Mid-east struggle as the provocateur of that "final" war (in Christian mythological thinking) is unknown. It is true that many faiths believe in a final judgment end of the world, but not with the same fervor and political power today as in American Fundamentalism. Further, American Fundamentalism is focused on the Middle East as the place that sparks that "Glorious Appearing" which will happen, soon! All warnings for 2000 years have been that these are the "Last" Days!

---

[23] These are not "Biblical" except by inference. That is, there is no direct Biblical reference to these, as there is to the poor. Helping the poor is clearly "Biblical." "Loving your enemy," is clearly Biblical but so is "killing your enemy." For instance, in Deuteronomy 20:10–20 "God" says to "put all the (enemy) males to the sword and take as your booty the women, children, livestock."

[24] Actually, the Lowy Institute in Australia contrasted Islamic fundamentalism with American foreign policy in terms of which is the, "…greatest threat to the world today." Australians were evenly divided about that. According to Raymond Bonner reporting from Sydney Australia on March 28, 2005, "…the Lowy Institute for International Policy (is a) research institute with a generally center-right orientation." New York Times, March 29, 2005.

The task of scholarship in Fundamentalism is to prove the given fundamentals. For instance, fundamentalist archaeologists go to Mt. Ararat to *find* Noah's Ark and to Jericho to prove the literal story, whereas other Biblical archaeologists, freed of fundamentalist assumptions, dig for whatever evidence they can find of the historicity of the stories. They are not trying to prove or disprove the story of Joshua and the walls of Jericho, or of Noah and the flood. Rather, they are seekers of the truth of *how* their faith stories came to be and what actually happened in the unfolding of history and in the expression of faith.

Dietrich Bonhoeffer, who died in one of Hitler's concentration camps, put it this way:

> It became increasingly clear to me that one achievement of so-called liberal theology has to be defended with great religious, ethical and scientific passion; namely, the right and duty of philological-historical criticism of the biblical literature without any condition except integrity of research and scientific honesty. Any dogmatic interference with this work would drive us into new or old superstitions—myths and symbols not understood as myths and symbols—and, since this cannot be done without the unconscious suppression of sounder knowledge, to fanaticism.

I'm suggesting that we get *unstuck* from Christian literalism or fundamentalism and the belief that "I possess the only *truth*" which leads to fanaticism—the precursor, according to Bonhoeffer, of fascism. Fundamentalism is a terrorism of the mind–a threat to both individual growth and democracy.

The Niagara Bible Conferences and Presbyterian General Assembly were a modern attempt to define right thinking (or orthodoxy). Like the conferences in the early centuries of the church, when creeds were formulated, books were selected to be included (or not) in the New Testament, and the Trinity was developed, this was conservative Protestants' attempt to define—and thus contain, protect, and control—Christianity. With the hundredth anniversary of the General Assembly coming soon, fundamentalists can celebrate. They are quite successful in America. The movement towards theocracy seems stronger now than at any time since our founding.

The fundamentalists were not, however, successful with my parents who, though they never drifted far from those five tenets of fundamentalism, still refused to accept the literalness of it all. They argued against what they perceived as blind dogmatism when pressured by others in their family and church. In this way, they were pretty "unstuck"!

Why free oneself from literalism? Because being stuck in the literalistic beliefs of our childhood—from Jonah and the whale to Santa and the tooth fairy—is similarly adolescent. Such beliefs are immature, not fully formed, not reasoned and certainly not our own. But there are other reasons as well.

First of all, literalism isn't really possible. There is no such thing. *All words are interpreted.* As you read this, you are interpreting in your own unique way. It is an illusion to think otherwise. Integrity in research demands that we scientifically study our origins—our scriptures—and understand the difference between faith and facts.

Second, literalism invites "inconsistency." How many literalists believe "Thou shalt not kill"? Few. (Quakers and Jehovah's Witnesses do.) Literalists will rationalize it for you, even though it's one of the Ten Commandments. They'll quote another scripture that contradicts it without batting an eye, and decry abortion while supporting the death penalty.

How many literalists keep holy the Sabbath, which is one of the Ten Commandments? (The Seventh Day Adventists do.) Again, hear the rationalizations for not doing so from others.

How many literalists abide by Jesus' admonition to "love your enemies" and "turn the other cheek"?

How many literalists follow the Apostle Paul's admonition to Timothy:[25] "I permit no woman to teach or to have authority over a man." Or his statements to the church at Corinth that a woman must wear a veil when she prays?[26]

The word "homosexual" and the word "abortion" are not mentioned in the Bible, and yet for many literalists, these are two primary moral values issues which they claim are Biblical. The references in Genesis 19[27] are used to support the literalists' claim about homosexuality per se and could, perhaps, only by a wild stretch of the imagination, be inferred to support a ban on gay marriage. They more clearly support a father giving his virgin daughters to strangers for sexual pleasure to protect his guests. Jesus seemed much more concerned about the poor, the rich (who will find entering the Kingdom harder than going through the eye of a needle), and the self-righteous. He didn't mention gays.

Literalists choose certain scriptures to support their beliefs and to explain away those which they don't accept. So do non-literalists—but they admit it! Literalism is an illusion, and therefore any religion built on it is also an illusion.

Life also is a mystery. Faith is a leap into an unknown and unproven place beyond certainty. We must get "unstuck" from superstition, free ourselves from the conflict between faith and science, and have enough confidence to live serenely in a chaotic and insecure world without being spoon-fed the "right" answers. This means having the courage to search within for one's own essence, one's own meaning, rather than uncritically accepting what is offered by others.

---

[25] I Timothy 2:11

[26] I Corinthians, Chapter 11

[27] This chapter focuses on hospitality more than homosexuality. Literalists must explain verses 7–9 "I beg you brothers, [who had requested the male guests, apparently for sexual reasons] look, I have two daughters who have not known [had sex with] a man; let me bring them out to you, and do to them as you please; only do nothing to these men, for they have come under the shelter of my roof."

The Gods Have Fallen

The gods have fallen
The world is round
The faithful listen
There is no sound
But the ever-shifting ground.

Where, oh where, may truth be found?
First, truth itself must go through fire
Be purged of the romance desire
That it be consummate and pure
False promises that reassure
This embossed version shall endure!
Then, only then, can truth be found
Ironically—on shifting ground.
The deep, deep sigh for you, for me
Comes when we quit so frantically
Chasing goblins for The Word
And find our peace in the absurd.
For truth, like standing on the sand
… ankle deep, twixt sea and land
Is beauty, fear, tide in, tide out
A swell of joy, a pang of doubt.

CHAPTER SIX: BIBLICAL?

*T*he following is by Rick Warren, the author of *The Purpose-Driven Life*, and is taken from his webpage. He has 60,000 subscribers and provided "Ministry Toolboxes" to "136,000 pastors"[28] before the 2004 U.S. elections. He writes:[29]

As church leaders, we know our congregations are not allowed to endorse specific candidates, and it's important for us to recognize that there can be multiple opinions among Bible-believing Christians when it comes to debatable issues such as the economy, social programs, Social Security, and the War in Iraq.

But for those of us who accept the Bible as God's Word and know that God has a unique sovereign purpose for every life, I believe there are five issues that are non-negotiable. To me, they're not even debatable, because God's Word is clear on these issues. In order to live a purpose-driven life—to affirm what God has clearly stated about his purpose for every person he creates—we must take a stand by finding out what the candidates believe about these five issues, and then vote accordingly.

Here are five questions to ask when considering who to vote for in this election:

1. What does each candidate believe about abortion and protecting the lives of unborn children?

2. What does each candidate believe about using unborn babies for stem-cell harvesting?

3. What does each candidate believe about homosexual "marriage"?

---

28 Warren's statement on PBS.
29 From "Why every U.S. Christian Must Vote in this Election" by Rick Warren on
www.purposedrivenlife.com.

4. What does each candidate believe about human cloning?

5. What does each candidate believe about euthanasia—the killing of elderly and invalids?

If these are the key questions for "Bible-believing Christians," are they truly Biblical? No! But are they okay to believe? Yes, quite assuredly! Is "God's Word" clear on these issues? Not at all! In fact, none of these is even mentioned in the Bible. None was a contemporary issue to the hundreds of authors whose writings contributed to the eventual compilation that Jews and Christians call "The Bible." They simply reflect a belief system, and that's certainly an acceptable thing to do.

As one might expect from writing that reflects a belief system, you may recognize bias in these questions (just as I'm sure you've already noted the bias in my writing!), especially in the definition of euthanasia. Webster defines it as "… method of causing death painlessly, so as to end suffering." A contrasting set of truly Biblical questions might look like this:

1. What does each candidate believe about love? Love is mentioned 500 times in the Bible.

2. What does each candidate believe about the poor and what action will he take? There are 225 Biblical references to the poor. (The number of poor people has now risen 17% under Mr. Bush)[30].

These next two are offered, "tongue in cheek." Of course, I would not vote for a candidate who approved of these – but *they are Biblical* reflecting, as scriptures do, the cultural views of that patriarchal time. Ethical decisions can be influenced by ancient writings but not limited by them.

---

[30] Kristof, Nicholas September 6, 2005 New York Times.

3. What does each candidate believe about the reinstitution of slavery or, at least, crystallizing a servant class? Even the Ten Commandments assume slavery—see Exodus 20:17—and countless verses recognize a servant/slave class and support the status quo. (Lev. 25:44-46, Ephesians 6:5)

4. What does each candidate believe about women? Does he support Ephesians 3:22-24 which clearly states that women should be subject to their husbands and I Corinthians 11:5-7 which states that women should wear veils when praying and I Corinthians 14:34-35 which makes clear that "Women should be silent in the churches. For they are not permitted to speak, but should be subordinate, as the law also says. If there is anything they desire to know, let them ask their husbands. For it is shameful for a woman to speak in church."

5. What does each candidate believe about the Ten Commandments, especially "Thou shalt not kill"? (Inclusion of this could support some of Warren's so-called Biblical questions by inference, just as it supports anti-war activists.)

Let me be *very* clear, again, that I am not endorsing the third and fourth Biblical questions I have just listed, but am calling attention to both the misuse of the word "Biblical," and to the fact that even when it is in the Bible it is not therefore necessarily ethical by modern standards. I protest this use by Christians in America just as Muslims protest their militant fundamentalists' attempt to take over the faith of Islam.

To use the commandment "Thou shalt not kill" only in reference to one social position (abortion) and not another (war) is an inconsistent use of the verse. It's okay to be inconsistent ("A foolish consistency is the hobgoblin of small minds," says Emerson) but to claim that your application is Biblical and the other is not—and, further, that your opponent is a murderer—violates the commandment that says "Thou shalt not bear false witness against your neighbor" (Exodus 20:16).

Anti-war protestors call those that support war "murderers." Abortionists do the same with opponents. Each has their deeply felt beliefs. Each has their "faith." When either claims that their faith is "God's Biblical Word" and that the other's is not, they have gone beyond what a human can know and have misled others into thinking that the Bible specifically, rather than inferentially, supports their cause. This is a misrepresentation. And, please note, *both* ends of the political spectrum are guilty of it.

Why do we do this? What I think is going on is that many people need to hold on to some authority outside themselves. Having faith without proof is too much for many. So they create the illusion of proof and confuse facts with faith. True faith needs no proof.

The ethical issues important to me—and, I believe, to the planet—are those about war and peace, poverty, the environment, and justice. The Bible offers no specific guidance on these for our time.

The newly elected (by a narrow margin) President of the United States Conference of Catholic Bishops is Bishop William Skylstad of Spokane, Washington. He is "… considered a liberal within the church because he sometimes emphasizes issues like poverty, the death penalty, and war, as well as abortion." In addition to the abortion issue, he posed "… questions to take into the voting booth about health care, peace, religious bigotry and other issues…" According to William Donohue, president of the conservative Catholic League, "There is this fight between the social justice and the pro-life sides of the Catholic Church."[31]

---

[31] From "Catholic Bishops, After a Divisive Debate, Choose a New Leader" by David D. Kirkpatrick, appearing in The New York Times on November 16, 2004.

Similarly, for me and for many other Americans, our faith points us in specific personal and political directions. Can those agendas or directions be inferred from the scriptures of the various religions? Absolutely! Can the specific directions be proven? Absolutely not! And this is what separates the literalists from other Christians.

Further, we answer the question, "Do you believe in the Bible?" rather differently than do the literalists. Our response would be "What a nonsensical question!" It's like asking, "Do you believe in Shakespeare or Robert Frost?"

The Bible is a collection of sixty-six (eighteen more when you total those in the Roman Catholic, Greek, and Slavonic Bibles that are not in Protestant Bibles) books or, actually, booklets written and edited by many different authors. They include poems (Psalms).

What does it mean to believe or not believe a poem?

There are parables (stories told to illustrate a point) and fables such as the story about men who build the tower of Babel to reach the heavens which, were the earth flat, would of course be up! In this story, God intervenes by having each of the builders begin to speak in a different language. Thus different languages are created! What a wonderful story.

When one "believes" the Bible, does that mean that he actually accepts that story as the beginning of language and actually believes one could build a structure high enough to reach heaven? (Heaven is written about elsewhere in this book.) If he disbelieves this story literally, must he throw it out of the Bible? Or ignore the whole Bible? When one says "I believe the Bible" does that mean he believes that giants once lived on earth[32], that men lived hundreds of years (nearly 1,000 for Methuselah)?

And how did these "books" become the Bible? The formulation evolved over several centuries and was eventually settled for

---

[32] Genesis 6:4

Christians in the fourth century. After being influenced over time by some powerful leaders, bishops from across the Roman Empire seeking orthodoxy (right beliefs) accepted the New Testament's twenty-seven books, thereby keeping out countless others. So why are these twenty-seven to be believed and the others *not* to be believed? To accept these twenty-seven is not an act of faith but rather of compliance to orthodoxy, or right belief, as determined by a group of men in the fourth century—nearly 350 years after Jesus lived.

It does not make sense to believe a book. You might believe what you think it means. The scriptures of mankind are a marvelous collection of wisdom. Perhaps you want to add the word "inspired" before the word "wisdom". So be it. But humans are the vehicles. Words, in the limited language of the writer, are the medium.

I read from scriptures often. I love the myths, poetry, and wisdom. I am enchanted and enriched. My favorite verse (which I also apply to my strongly held opinions) is "He who thinks he knows, knows not. He who thinks he does not know, knows." This is from the Upanishads, an ancient written scripture from India.

My advice is to believe in *life*—not a book. Do not get stuck on words in the scriptures as if they mean only one thing. See through your favorite scriptures to the meaning beyond. Let them be transparent. Imagine that you could hold up your favorite scriptures, like a crystal glass, and see through them to the sun and the stars. Then you may know what Meister Eckhart meant in the 13th century when he said, "In order to find God you must let go of god!" That is, don't be stuck on your ethnic secondhand childhood definition of God/Goddess. Go beyond that.

One way to do this is to move beyond the definition of myth as "false" and understand the value of myth, and particularly the role it plays in the Bible. Let's start with the word "myth."

Mythos (or myth) in its deeper meaning is the language of the gods (to put it poetically). That is, of the various ways to write or speak about the mystery of life, myths are the most profound way to communicate that which cannot be communicated (the "indescribable" or "ineffable"). Perhaps this is because myths often arise from our unconscious, the place from which dreams come. Poetry (psalms), fiction (like Jonah in the Hebrew scriptures), parables (short, pointed stories often ascribed to Jesus), and visions (as in the story of Daniel or the New Testament Book of Revelation) are also profound ways to speak or write about the primal energy and source of life.

The problem arises when one takes any of these expressions as a literal event. Children literalize stories (think Santa). Adults put away childish literalism and look beyond or through the stories to deeper meanings.

Take the Garden of Eden myth. If you literalize it, then you accept that there were these two people who talked with God, talked to a snake (which stood erect), ate from a tree which gave them knowledge of good and evil, and then, encouraged by the snake, cast their eyes on the Tree of Life. The Lord God said, "See, the man has become like one of us, knowing good and evil; and now he might reach out his hand and take also from the Tree of Life, and eat, and live forever." So God cast them from the Garden of Eden (Genesis 3:11).

All ancient peoples told their own story of Creation. Understanding origins has always intrigued us. Some Native American stories tell of the first humans emerging up from the earth (think Mother Earth) in their present adult form. Other equally marvelous stories abound. The Garden of Eden story is one of these (Genesis 2-5).

The Garden of Eden myth finds first man (Adam) and first woman (Eve—created from a rib of Adam) living in paradise. Told by God not to eat fruit from the tree, they do what is forbidden after being chided by the serpent: "Don't pay attention to that rule. Nothing will happen!"

So they eat. The knowledge of good and evil thereby enters the world. The snake must now crawl on it's belly. Man must labor, and woman must bear children. Dualism is established—that is, Good God/Bad God (Satan) and Good and Evil. Adam and Eve are expelled from the Garden and have three sons. One (Cain) kills another (Abel), at which point Cain is sent to the land of Nod, East of Eden, where he finds a wife. (See Genesis Chapter 4). If you take this literally, you must, to be consistent, answer a few questions:

When did God quit talking to people and why?

If Adam and Eve were the first people, how was there a wife (in the land of Nod) for Cain? The next son, Seth, also has a son. Where did his wife come from?

Where is this Garden of Eden? Is it at the joining of the Tigris and Euphrates Rivers, as some traditions claim? If so, how do you reconcile the claims of current science that all humans come out of Africa (according to Stanford University DNA studies), and the likelihood that the migration to the Middle East happened tens of thousands of years later?[33]

Literal interpretations lead us into futile arguments of true–false and likely miss the deeper meaning of the mythos (myths) of all scriptures of the world. So, we need to search for the personal, deeper meaning in the symbolism, to give it relevance in our own lives. Going back to the Garden of Eden myth:

Guarding the entrance to the Garden are two cherubim with flaming swords (Genesis 3:24). In mythic understanding, and also in the meaning the myth takes on for me, the two cherubim or dragon-like creatures represent fear and desire.

I think, "Fear of death! Fear of loss of wealth. Fear of strangers. Fear of whatever."

---

[33] The Journey of Man—a PBS documentary.

I think, "Desire for more! Desire for wealth. Desire for another's property. Desire for fame."

Picture yourself, along with me, outside the Garden entrance. Picture the cherubim waving the flaming swords. Face the entrance! When you will give up fear and desire, you may calmly walk past the swords into the Garden! What a moment. I write "moment" because I have experienced such moments, only then to become afraid or to want that which I do not have, and then find myself swiftly outside the Garden again. In this mythic journey, I kick myself out of the Garden or I move myself past desire and fear into the Garden again.

This process of interpretation, this reaching to discover the deeper meanings of these stories, is the forerunner of faith! Literalism ties itself to the attempt to prove ancient stories as historical. Faith is beyond such alleged "proof." With proof, one need not have faith. Both faith and hope are a dynamic leap into the unknown, into living-without-knowing-for-sure. There is no rational proof in these realms. Such faith/hope is an act of courage.

It's an exciting journey to wake up to every day, embracing this sort of faith. It is also ever so much more liberating and challenging for me than a literal reading of the Garden of Eden or other Ancient stories.

CHAPTER SEVEN: MYTHS AND MORE MYTHS

One way to think about the Garden of Eden and other stories in the Bible is to ask, "What is the opposite of literal?" In language and story-telling, there are a number of possibilities: metaphoric, poetic, symbolic, allegorical. These terms refer to ways of describing reality that point to another "level" of meaning beyond the words and events of the story. Metaphors and allegories use language at one level of meaning, e.g., the snake in the Garden, to point to larger meanings, e.g., Satan or evil, as a sort of subtext for the story. An allegory often tells a tale at a literal level (Jonah and the whale) and can be enjoyed fully at that level. However, the real story exists at another, symbolic level (good and evil, right and wrong).

The Bible contains all forms of literature, mixing history and myth with points of view about faith. Myths present allegories about our origins and explanations of natural phenomena. All peoples seem to have some kind of "origin" myth, including stories about the births of their greatest leaders and holy men, the "special" people.

Virgin Births

Consider the *virgin birth* of Jesus' story. And of the Buddha. And of countless other spiritual leaders, Divine Beings and shamen in Mideastern, Greek, Native American and other cultures. And consider the function of Mythos.

Christians versed in their New Testament know that Jesus died in about the year 29 A.D. The Apostle Paul—the preeminent early definer of the new faith—wrote from about 50 to 60 A.D. He never mentions the virgin birth. Maybe he never heard the story, or didn't believe it, or thought it irrelevant. But he never mentioned it.

The first and only recording of this birth are in the Gospels of Matthew and Luke (and these stories differ) in about the years 80–85 A.D., fifty years after the death and, it's said, the resurrection of Jesus.

As early Christianity moved from a Jewish sect (after all, Jesus and his disciples, family and friends were Jewish) into the Greek world, the emergence of a virgin birth story makes sense. Many Greek gods were born of a union of one of the gods with a human woman. Though not compatible with Jewish miracle births, a virgin birth placed Jesus in the company of the divine as the early Christians entered the non-Jewish world.

A Jewish miracle birth was conception in old age between humans. "God said to Abraham … I will bless her [Sarah] and give you a son by her … . Abraham fell on his face and laughed, and said to himself, 'Can a child be born to a man who is a hundred years old? Can Sarah, who is ninety years old, bear a child?'"[34] Isaac was born in this remarkable story.[35]

Native Americans tell stories of virgin births. There are stories of Buddha being born out of the hip of his mother. These stories are frequent and found in ancient lore around the world. Special people are born in special ways.

I believe that you and I are special, too. And so, for me, the virgin birth is a metaphor—a myth—about you and me embracing and drinking in our own specialness. When we do so, we are reborn—not by biological conception—but by spiritual conception. All creation is accepted—the leaf, the flower, and on and on. So am I. So are you. The leaf and the flower don't think their way into their acceptance. Neither can we. We simply must accept it. The leaf and the flower aren't aware and can't celebrate, but we can.

---

[34] Genesis 17:16–17. Also read Genesis 18:9-15.

[35] Abraham previously had a son, Ishmael, by Hagar, the slave, about whom God promised, "I will make him a great nation." Ishmael, the first-born, is to Islam (Muslims) what Isaac is to Hebrews. Muslims believe that Islam is the religion of the descendants of Isma'il (Arabic spelling).

The Devil Made Me Do It

The Devil is … well, an interesting idea at the very least. It flourished after Zoroaster (centuries before the Christian era) posited a god of light and a god of darkness. Thus, we can believe that evil is caused outside oneself, and the good god is innocent of any complicity in the matter! It's that bad god—the devil!

Nice try. And a very good selling job. Millions of people claiming belief in one god buy this two-god notion. In the last decade, two popular married fundamentalist evangelists who were caught in adulterous relationships blamed the devil and reaped rewards of both sympathy and money from their followers.

What's closer to the truth is that you and I create joy and sorrow, good and bad.

Nobody else.

No good or bad god.

Some baseball players, when they hit a home run, point up (to a god in the heavens, I suppose, as though some deity deserves credit). Where is the pitcher supposed to point? Down?

Good and evil come from you and me—from us.

Actually, that puts us in charge, which is a great idea … but tough, sometimes.

Heaven and Hell

As those baseball players on a flat earth know, Heaven is up; Hell is down. Both are recent concepts—perhaps written about only 2,500 years ago, and even then they were undeveloped ideas, dissimilar from the way people think of them today.

Pre-historic humans first began to bury their dead with artifacts (suggesting a notion of afterlife) some 80,000 years ago. By comparison, it is estimated that "humans" have been on earth, in an earlier form, for perhaps 4,000,000 years.

All of the scriptures were written when humans believed that the earth was flat. The heavens were fixed lights that could be reached by building a high enough tower, and the sun was pulled across the sky by chariots. Some of the gods lived on the highest mountains; others lived among the creatures of the earth or in the earth itself. The Norse gods lived in Valhalla.

In Judaism, the idea gradually developed that the dead descended beneath the surface of this flat earth to a nondescript abode called Hades. In Egypt, families and provisions were buried with the Pharaoh, assuming a future life. A few good men ascended to the heavens, which were not far away, to enjoy a "new" life. And eventually the myth grew to where there were three levels of heaven and then seven. Thus the saying, "seventh heaven."

Hades, on the other hand, evolved to a three-sectioned place which was <u>not</u> the fiery hell of 13th century Dante (*The Divine Comedy*) but a misty abode of the dead. The Book of Revelation in the Christian New Testament further developed the notion of Hades. In our current understanding, it makes less sense that heaven would be "up" and hell would be "down" because we live on a round earth. Perhaps hell can make sense if the center of the earth is hot.

Heaven is more difficult to reconcile with modern knowledge. Ascending to a heaven at the edge of the universe even at the speed of light would be a very long journey. But perhaps the soul, separated from the body, can be beamed up. Imagine your last words being "Beam me up." Or, as suggested to me by a grandson, perhaps we live in parallel universes, with heaven running through the very space we are now standing in.

But beyond the flat earth/round earth dilemma lies a deeper problem. In the vast scheme of Creation, does it seem reasonable— if there is an afterlife—that it will only be for those of my own religion or that those who do not worship and believe as I do will either not attain life after death or will burn in Hell?

*Heaven—*After *Life?*

Elsewhere, I have written about the confining beliefs of childhood. Among them are our beliefs about Heaven and Hell, what they are like, who gets to go where and when.

I believe that Heaven is now. *Est!* Now.

The Medieval mystic Meister Eckhart wrote, "Your state here is your eternal state. This is hell or heaven." Why do we waste our lives waiting for after-life? Living in the future means to be dead to the present, here-and-now moment. We can choose to live fully in the now—vibrantly aware, as we would be upon seeing a doe suddenly cross our path.

Most people are only "pulled" into the present—and now—by a tragedy, a birth, or a major life event. *This* is the moment. There is no other. One can only live or be unconscious. To be fully present now is to experience Heaven.

This is the Garden. This is paradise. This is the Holy land—the Holy place. *Questo momento e' la vostra vita* (This moment is your life.) Embrace!

The Eternal Now: A Parable

I have lived in very bleak circumstances. The streets of my city were made of gold. Choirs sang cherubic music all day—all night. Nobody aged. My mother remained 23 all her life. By request I became 25—forever. All my needs were granted. There was no illness. My bones never ached.

Nobody cried. No tears were shed at parting, for we knew that we would never part. No sorrow. No anger. I loved that life. I don't know how long this happiness lasted–time was not measured there. But at some point I slowly began to experience what you mortals call "boredom."

The first time I felt it—boredom—a voice spoke to me as if from a giant loudspeaker. "Robert, discipline yourself. This is a place of great joy. Do not dwell on joyless feelings."

Somebody knew my unspoken thoughts! But the feeling increased, and I soon was instructed to stop at a discipline care center. I hadn't noticed that there was one on every corner.

They gave me a small tablet, in a gold wrapper. "One a day," said these lovely winged creatures.

I don't know how long it took, but finally I realized that the problem wasn't me; the problem was the place. Perhaps the result of a bad pill. Whatever the cause, I was now awake, but the alternatives were bleak. Since we were immortal, suicide was not an option. Instead, I searched for others like me. There were many of us visiting the discipline care centers daily. A small group of us began to meet (undetected, we thought) and dreamed of another life where:

> *…Seeds grew and died.*

> *…People aged.*

> *…All things ended.*

> *…Everyone knew that each moment was transient and, therefore, precious.*

> *…Cities weren't golden but were what we created them to be.*

> *…People cried and laughed, hated and loved.*

> *…There was pain, suffering and unwanted killing.*

> *…We would be the creators of our own lives!*

But we were detected. Our punishment was to be sent to this "heaven" of our fantasy—planet Earth.

And every moment I am here, I realize that to be fully present now is the immortality I dreamed of. There is no further shore. I inhale each precious moment knowing that it is transient. I walk on dirt, grass and sidewalks instead of gold. (The gold never interested me much— it's hard, cold and inert.)

Occasionally, by mistake, I turn my car radio dial to a station as a voice is saying "Are you ready for the streets of gold?" and "He knows your every thought." And I shudder!

Here Comes Santa Claus

It may seem a little irreverent to follow on a discussion of Heaven and Hell with the myth of Santa Claus. However, this very ancient myth, which predates Christianity by tens of thousands of years, provides an excellent way to illustrate the spiritual journey from the literalism of childhood to deeper mythic meanings.

Almost universally, children literalize stories. So Santa is real, lives at the North Pole, makes gifts year round, rides in a sleigh and has time (and appetite) to drink all the hot chocolate and eat all the cookies laid out for him with such care while covering the whole world in a single night! A wonderful story and belief.

But gradually—or suddenly as in my case—the story unravels.

At the age of six or seven an older child told me there was *no* real Santa! I was devastated. (To this day I believe I remember the very location where I was told this!) My parents tenderly confirmed this new information. I believed that Christmas was ruined for me forever!

Of course, gradually I discovered the joy of giving until, as a father, I experienced this joy with my literal little children and then again with them as emerging adults. I like receiving gifts, but I love giving them.

The mythic meaning of the Santa story is much, much richer than my simple childhood beliefs would have suggested.

I am Santa. I am Santa's helper. And I experience my inner child's joy when I receive a gift. The Santa story is no longer "out there." It is in "here." I recreate it. I live it! Daily.

Little did I realize as a child that the same wonderful journey "from the North Pole" lay ahead for me as I moved from my childhood literal beliefs in my religious teachings to a deeper, mythic, spiritual understanding.

It is painful to me when I meet an older person who still claims to believe literally what they believed as a child. It is equally painful to meet an adult who has rejected off-handedly those tales and who has not discovered the deep meanings in the ancient stories of the various faith traditions. Rejecting the mythic stories is as absurd as rejecting Shakespeare because he wrote fiction or rejecting poetry because it isn't factual.

We are stuck in our secondhand learning if we retain the literal beliefs of our childhood. We are also stuck if we reject them offhand without mining them. We must learn from and respect our heritage and then go beyond it.

Myth is the closest we can get to the mystery of Life. I hope you will embrace its multiplicity and nuance as you find your own meanings in life. Be Santa. Be in (and out of) the Garden. Simply—be.

And remember that ...

"It ain't necessarily so.

The things that you're liable

To read in the Bible

They ain't necessarily so."[36]

Yes!

It Ain't!

But when it ain't to be taken literally, there's a
      deeper meaning.

Find it.

Others have written about it.

Read them.

But find yours!

---

[36] From "Porgy and Bess" by George Gershwin.

CHAPTER EIGHT: GOD'S WORD AND THE LIMITS OF LANGUAGE

Originally, there were grunts, sighs, coos, clicks, screams. These were the sounds of humans. As they moved—even from one valley to the next—the sounds evolved into different "languages."

Now—as then—all sounds, words, gestures, and tones are interpreted in many different ways, and our ability to communicate clearly is limited. Words intended to convey a certain message are received in different ways by different people participating in the same conversation. As you read this page you will understand its words differently than will another reader. Even seemingly descriptive words like "green" have many different meanings and interpretations. If you need more paint to finish painting your house, would you call the store and simply order more "green paint" expecting to get the same shade?

Words are also circular. Look up a word in the dictionary, and you will be guided to yet another word that helps define it. Eventually you will be guided back to your first word.

Words point many directions. "Green" can point to certain frequencies of light in the color spectrum. It can also refer to someone who is inexperienced. It can also suggest envy. Thus, a single word may have many meanings. There are its *denotative* meanings which are its explicit or direct meanings ("home—a place where one lives"), and then there are the *connotative* or associative meanings ("home—a place of warmth and affection") which are suggested by the word. Given the complexity of communicating with someone who speaks the *same* language, imagine all the difficulties in translating from one language to another—particularly from an ancient language to a modern one. Translating connotative meanings is extremely difficult. This explains the volumes written by Biblical scholars on the exact meanings of Biblical texts. These experts report that 25% of the Hebrew words in The Torah (Genesis, Exodus, Leviticus, Numbers, and Deuteronomy) have interpretations that are disputed within their scholarly community.

Thus, to say that you *believe literally* the words of the Bible makes no sense. Some believers want to read their sacred scriptures in that original tongue believing it is as God dictated it. Even when read in the original language, people differ on scriptural meanings. And once any of the original texts are translated, their meanings have necessarily been altered by the translators' judgments. So even if the ancient texts contain the exact words of God, as some fundamentalists claim, you can be sure that the translations do not!

All translation is interpretation. What do you suppose that "original language" was anyway? Does God have a language? Is it Arabic (Koran)? Sanskrit (Hindu)? Hebrew (Jewish)? Aramaic (Christian)? Mandarin? Farsi? Early African? Native-American? Latin?

It is an illusion to think you can read the words of God. If you think these words are literal and the beliefs they (supposedly) convey explain the mystery of life, then you worship words as idols. Words can never explain life, death, or destiny. No words can contain the indescribable mystery that is Life. If indeed there is "objective" reality, you and I can never know it. Our view of reality is limited to our opinions, beliefs and thoughts—our perceptual screen.

All is translation.

All is interpretation.

All is impermanent.

The greater value is to see beyond the words to the infinite, which cannot be described with words. The words are only symbols pointing past themselves to the greater meanings that lie in each Self and often cannot be shared. We make sounds to each other, and each of us walks away with our own meaning.

The Word "God"

When we consider the meaning of the word "God," this is especially true. The English word has three letters but a multitude of meanings, and, therefore, one should never assume it means to others what it means to oneself. The various ideas of god/goddess are sometimes helpful if one doesn't take any particular definition too seriously.

After all, a definition is just a thought. Thoughts are words with multiple meanings. It is outrageous to think that any one definition of "god/goddess" can describe the indescribable ultimate mystery of our source of life and of continual energy.

Who dares to claim that they can put words together which will define this mystery? Who dares to claim that they or their holy book is the *only* one that has captured and defined that which is beyond definition?

There is a great void that, paradoxically, contains all of our unknowing. So be it. This void is filled—not with distinctions about god/goddess—but with existence-energy. And as a drop of water is one with the ocean but not the ocean, I am one with the existence. I am energy. I exist. I am at peace. There is no magical revelation. That I am one with all Experience—the same substance—*that* is the magic.

However, while the words "god/goddess" dwell in that magical connotative domain, there is a great deal of history behind the idea of a deity (or deities). Most deity artifacts found before the year 3000 B.C. were goddesses. For tens and probably hundreds of thousands of years humans worshipped goddesses. Even the sun (and certainly the moon) was feminine. When primitive man thought of Creation, birthing, nurturing, he thought "goddess"—feminine. We retain this in our language today when we refer to "Mother Earth." There were male deities as well but these did not come into prominence until about 4500 years ago when war for the purpose of conquering land began.

For eons, humans lived in survival mode against the elements of Nature and stronger animals. Humans needed other humans, and they gathered into clans for survival— to protect themselves, to find food and shelter through the cooperative efforts of clan members, and to defend themselves from outsiders. There was no agriculture, and since land was plentiful, there was no need to capture or protect it.

These cooperative efforts helped to wire the human nervous system for socialization and collaboration. We know that humans perform spontaneous acts of courage and risk their own lives to save strangers. Armies lament that many of their soldiers do not (cannot?) pull the trigger. However, others *do* pull the trigger, having been reconditioned by rigorous military training or when facing a clear threat to their family, community, group or self. Gradually, the goddesses who represented the feminine and generative aspects of humankind lost their influence to the gods—the fierce male gods who modeled power and conquest and/or provided a needed defense from others.

In the three dominant Western faiths (Judaism, Islam, Christianity) a storm god from the Arabian Peninsula came to represent power. Amazingly, all three religions adopted that same god: "Jahweh," "Jehovah," "Allah" and "God" all refer to the same god of Abraham, Ishmael, Isaac and Jacob.

Fundamentalists/Traditionalists in all three religions believe that this god favors them, and each claims that certain writings (the Hebrew Bible, the Koran and the New Testament) contain God's (or Jahweh's ["Jehovah"] or Allah's) words. In their extreme traditionalist/fundamentalist belief form, all three believe in a final Judgment Day which will prove one of them right against the other two. This final day is related to the belief (in various forms, of course) that a war will take place in the Middle East at which time the male god will intervene on their behalf.

The deep belief about this final outcome among the traditionalist and/or fundamentalists of these three religions is a force behind the resistance to peace in the Holy Land.[37] Such beliefs are not unusual at the highest levels of government in the United States, Israel, and various Middle Eastern countries (Iran and Saudi Arabia, for instance).

Giving definition to the "ultimate" being or source not only reduces the primal source to a variety of definitions invented by humans, but also sets those who accept one definition against those who believe in another. If you say "god," you imply "male." If you say goddess you imply "female." If you say "Jahweh" ("Jehovah"), you imply a different entity from "Allah," even though, in this case, they refer to the same god! You have defined or limited what ultimately cannot be defined. You have created (by your definition) a lesser god/goddess.

Primal energy or source is simply indescribable and indefinable. Even saying "primal energy" or "source" is limiting, but the generalized nature of these terms admits more interpretations than they exclude and therefore, for me, they are preferable to "god/goddess." The ultimate mystery will not be defined. *That's the way it is.*

Simply put—

There is existence.

All energy is existence.

You are one with existence!

Celebrate!

Those who are sure that they know God's very words should remember that "He who thinks he knows, knows not. He who thinks he does not know, knows." But what does he who does not know, know?

That you cannot, by words, know!

That there are no final answers that can be written.

---

37 Many other religions also believe in a last judgment and second coming. In Hinduism the tenth and last incarnation of Vishnu will be Kalkin appearing in order to judge sinners, save the righteous and usher in the Golden Age. He, like Jesus is often depicted with a white horse.

That there may be an answer, but it cannot be known by humans.

That if humans claim to possess in their sacred book or priestly self the answers, then they are claiming to be Deity, or rather, the Ultimate Being.

That to be in touch with reality is to know that the mystery of life is beyond words! Again quoting the 14th century Roman Catholic mystic Meister Eckhart, "The mind must be raised to an unknowing knowing."

That my knowing is intuitive, is within, is all I can or need to know.

Does this view lead to atheism? Not at all! Atheism is a sad, Life-sucking idea. It is a dis- or un-belief in God—but of which god? God has thousands of faces. Which one is the atheist rejecting? "I don't believe in God" is another nonsensical statement.

What about god/goddess as a first source—as the fundamental energy from which all come? Does the atheist believe there is no fundamental energy—nothing that provides an original spark? Can one imagine all the universes without some original, swirling, creating Energy out of which, eventually, we all have evolved? There is no getting around the fact that this elemental energy came from somewhere. I may call it "energy"; you may call it "God." The problem is that, having evolved a personality, humans have then often projected human features and personality onto their primitive and limiting notion of that energy and made it an article of belief. To reject this view, some would say, is to not believe in God.

Thus, atheism is a narrow disbelief in reaction to a narrow belief. Literalism is the misguided attempt to claim that your interpretation is the one and only correct truth. In this sense, literalism is the opposite of faith, which one posits without proof. Atheism is a reaction to the fundamentalist's God and is its polar opposite. But atheism is also as literalistic as the fundamentalist's view of God:

both views are held dogmatically, each resting on a narrowly defined conception of "God." Psychologically, they are the same in that they claim that they know the "truth."

Language and The Historical Jesus

The limitation of language is also true, of course, of the words of Jesus, who, the New Testament says, taught us to pray "Our Father, who art in Heaven … ." This is a familiar phrase for Christians. It is a 17th century translation from the Latin, copied over and over by monks for centuries after being translated into Latin from Greek. These words are attributed to Jesus, who spoke in Aramaic, a language still spoken in parts of the Middle East.

Arabic is the popular language of the Arab world today and is the sacred language of the Koran, the scriptures that Muslims believe were revealed to Mohammed, the prophet of Islam. Some believe it is the language of Allah himself. "Allah" is the Arabic word for "Deo" and "God." The word Jesus used was "Allaha."

The script for Aramaic and Arabic is radically different from English. Translation is a very difficult task and much can be lost across the centuries and across several languages (as is the case here), especially since translators are biased by a particular theological way of thinking. Translators must make difficult decisions, which is why translations differ.

For instance, whereas in the First century Christian church men and women seem to equally share priestly functions, by the Second century a strong patriarchy had emerged—and only men became priests in the evolving Church. The idea of God-as-Father supported the way the church was being re-structured and would encourage translators to write "Our Father" rather than "Oh Birther" as Neil Douglas-Klotz believes the Aramaic should be translated.

Were we reading the "Our father who art in heaven" phrase translated by Douglas-Klotz directly from the Aramaic, it would read "O Birther, father-mother of the Cosmos." Now, Douglas-Klotz is also a translator with *his* theological biases! We cannot avoid the fact that all is interpreted! Every word that you read here is being interpreted through your filtering systems—your beliefs—your biases. But suppose Christians were praying "O Birther" rather than "Our Father." Does this seem different to you? Likewise, does "cosmos" strike you differently than "Heaven"?

Thus, we don't truly *know* what the words of Jesus were, despite the fact that Christian scholars have been seeking to understand Jesus the man for centuries. Since about 1850 serious scholarship has taken place—especially in Europe and America. One such scholar was Albert Schweitzer, the great organist, theologian and medical doctor, who spent most of his adult life in Africa providing Western medical services to the people. In 1898 as referenced earlier, his work "The *Quest for the Historical Jesus*" burst like a bomb on the European religious scene. For a decade he was forbidden to preach to the African people.

Actually many scholars preceded him in this quest to cut through the traditional theology to find the real Jesus—with his brothers and sisters and mother and father and life as a child and adolescent. These scholars' recounting would go like this:

He lived.

He wrote nothing.

He died in the year 29.

Stories were told.

Paul (the apostle) wrote letters to Christians 20 to 30 years later.

During this period, it was common to hear stories about extraordinary miracles performed by heroes and heroines that were told and believed across the world, and many religions celebrated the death and resurrection of a god. Such stories were very familiar in Jesus' time. Christians believed he had survived death but had many differing ideas about how. They felt his presence. Paul said he appeared "in" him, equating this with other stories of Jesus' resurrection. Others said "to" them, that is, he "appeared" to them. However different the stories, the storytellers say they felt a profound difference in their lives.

About the year 65 A.D., a gospel (good news) was written and ascribed to Mark. Scholars believe that some individuals wrote notes about Jesus that were later gathered in a document called quelle (source) or Q. In about 80 A.D., Luke and Matthew wrote their gospels, and later John did so, all using the source "Q."

Many other writings, including small books, emerged late in the First century attributing vastly different theologies to this man Jesus. A number of these texts were hidden to avoid destruction by other Christians. (In 1945, they—the Nag Hammadi texts—were discovered in earthen jars.) In Luke and Matthew we read (for the first time) the Virgin Birth story—80 years after Jesus' birth. The earlier gospel of Mark doesn't mention it. So:

He lived

He died

He was remembered

He was experienced as a living presence to many.

He was interpreted in many different ways.

He was written about (decades later.)

He was doctrinized.

He became the source for a new religion.

The key question for me is: Can people of the 21st century have the same deep spiritual experience as the early Christians had—and as the Hebrews, Hindus, Muslims and many others before and since then had—in the original emergence of their faith?

Can the wisdom of the ages be embodied in you? Can it be experienced today? Can you, as in Joseph Campbell's poem[38],

> Find those levels in the psyche
>
> that open, open, open,
>
> and finally open to the mystery of your
> Self
>
> being Buddha consciousness or the
> Christ.

Or is this reserved for a special few?

In our search for the historical Jesus—the undoctrinized version of the life of this fellow whose birth heralds the end of B.C. and the beginning of A.D.—there is often a fear that the (physical) flesh-and-blood Jesus will overshadow or somehow despoil the (spiritual) Christ. However, if we are not somehow *like* Jesus, how can his life have meaning for us?

After my divorce from the mother of my children I was single for six years. Struggling with the issue of relationships and sexuality during that period I wrote this poem:

Jesus, He was Single, Too

> I hadn't thought of him that way…
>
> he surely didn't have to face
>
> what I face nearly every day,
>
> or if he did, he clearly had
>
> a simple principle within:
>
> he'd feel the urge
>
> but not give in.
>
> For urges surely lead to wrong
>
> and are suppressed by someone strong
>
> or even worse, they don't belong,

---

[38] See complete poem on page 127.

they're not a part of you and me

if we have spirituality!

Suppose in Jesus body and soul

were always one—inseparable!

That those he loved, he loved to touch

and sometimes touched them very much

and sometimes he and they were one

like God, the Father, and the Son.

Would he mean any less to you

or more, perhaps,

if this were true?

A religious source (like Jesus) doesn't have to be like me for me to honor his or her gifts. But I have to believe they've faced some of the life dilemmas that I'm up against. And Evil for me isn't having or not having explicit sex activities. I think such a moralistic approach completely misses the point!

Jesus' life was a whole, unified event; it was not the life of Jesus on one hand and the designated title of "Christ" on the other. There is no splitting off of physical and spiritual, just as I am both a sexual being and a spiritual one. Jesus' sexuality is not a heretical idea.

Alexander Pushkin's poem "The Gabriliad" was considered heretical when it was censored by the Czar. As poets often do, this greatest Russian poet pushes the edge of orthodoxy by placing Mary, the mother of Jesus, in sexual situations with God, Gabriel, and the Devil. "I've had too many callers to be bored: Count them—all in one day I have been had by The Tempter, an Archangel, and the Lord."[39] Written in 1821, Pushkin denied his authorship of the poem until 1828. Poets and novelists exist to challenge the establishment and to help each of us think again and again.

---

[39] Alexander Pushkin 1799–1837

Given Margaret Starbird's work and Dan Brown's *The Da Vinci Code* someone has suggested that I rethink my poem. Perhaps, instead:

> Jesus, he was married too
>
> . I never thought of him that way!

Was Jesus a Literalist?

To conclude this chapter, I return to our central question about the meaning and implications of liberal, conservative and fundamentalist beliefs. By Biblical account, Jesus broke new ground by defying the literalists (Pharisees) of his day. The religious leaders found him to be dangerous. Was he a liberal, conservative, fundamentalist—or all three? Below, I present a number of "direct quotes" from Jesus and some stories from the New Testament. Using the definitions at the beginning of Chapter Five, you can decide for yourself. If my chosen selections seem skewed, then read for yourself the Gospels of Matthew, Mark, Luke and John.

> "Beware of practicing your piety before others in order to be seen by them." Matt 6:1

> "Do not store up for yourselves treasures on earth." Matt 6:19

> "When you give a banquet, invite the poor, the crippled, the lame, and the blind. And you will be blessed, because they cannot repay you, for you will be repaid at the resurrection of the righteous." Luke 14:13-14

> "You have heard that it was said 'You shall love your neighbor and hate your enemy.' But I say to you, Love your enemies and pray for those who persecute you." Matthew 5:43-44

> "Come to me, all you that are weary and are carrying heavy burdens, and I will give you rest." Matt 11:28

"At that time Jesus went through the grain fields on the Sabbath; his disciples were hungry, and they began to pluck heads of grain and to eat. When the Pharisees saw it, they said to him, 'Look, your disciples are doing what is not lawful to do on the Sabbath.'" Matt 12:1-2

"Give to everyone who begs from you; and if anyone takes away your goods, do not ask for them again. Do to others as you have them do to you." Luke 6:30-31

"Then Jesus said, 'Father forgive them, for they know not what they are doing.'" Luke 23:34

"Then Jesus said to him, 'Put your sword in its place; for all who take the sword will perish by the sword.'" Matt 26:52

"Sell your possessions and give the money to the poor." Matt 19:21

"It is easier for a camel to go through the eye of a needle than for someone who is rich to enter the kingdom of God." Matt 19:24

Jesus' disciples had gone to the city to buy food. "Jesus, tired out by his journey, was sitting by the well. It was about noon. A Samaritan woman came to draw water, and Jesus said to her, 'Give me a drink.' The Samaritan woman said to him, 'How is it that you, a Jew, ask a drink of me, a woman of Samaria?' [Jews do not share things with Samaritans.] Just then his disciples came. They were astonished that he was speaking with a woman." John 4:6-9 and 27

"On another Sabbath he entered the synagogue and taught, and there was a man there whose right hand was withered. The scribes and the Pharisees watched him to see whether he would cure on the Sabbath, so they might find an accusation against him. Even though he knew what they were thinking, he said to the man who had the withered hand, 'Come and stand here.' He got up and stood there. Then Jesus said to them, 'I ask you, is it lawful to do good or to do harm on the Sabbath, to save life or to destroy it?' After looking around at all of them, he said to him 'Stretch out your hand.' He did so, and his hand was restored. But they were filled with fury and discussed with one another what they might do to Jesus." Luke 6:6-11

"The scribes and the Pharisees brought a woman who had been caught in adultery: and making her stand before all of them, they said to him, 'Teacher, this woman was caught in the very act of committing adultery. Now in the law Moses commanded to stone such women. Now what do you say?' They said this to test him, so that they might have some charge to bring against him. Jesus bent down and wrote with his finger on the ground. When they kept on questioning him, he straightened and said to them, 'Let anyone among you who is without sin be the first to throw a stone at her.' John 8:3-7

"You have heard that it was said, 'An eye for an eye and a tooth for a tooth' but I say to you, Do not resist an evildoer. But if anyone strikes you on the right cheek, turn the other also; and if anyone wants to sue you and take your coat, give your cloak as well; and if anyone forces you to go one mile, go also the second mile. Give to everyone who begs from you." Matt 5:38-42

You can also read the story of the Good Samaritan (Luke 10:29-37) and the Prodigal son (Luke 15:11-32) and the story of

Jesus overturning the tables in the temple (Mark 11:15-18). You will see that Jesus, like other spiritual leaders (Moses, Amos, the Buddha, Mohammed, Zoroaster, and others) goes beyond rigid doctrines and challenges the establishment. When these leaders are gone, ironically, a new establishment creates an orthodoxy meant to protect and pass on what, for many, becomes a new rigid system of belief.

Was Jesus a liberal? Are present-day Christian literalists simply accepting the most current orthodoxy? What about religions claiming that their scriptures are literal? Quite simply, these claims do not change the fact that words are sophisticated sounds that are interpreted in different ways. What else explains the fact that there are so many differences in scriptural belief among even those who share the same religion?

Truth is one. Knowing this frees one from the tyranny and absolute power of doctrine—it frees one to engage deeply in all scriptures to find meaning far richer than what literalism can offer.

CHAPTER NINE: POLITICAL IMPLICATIONS

*T*o conclude this section on Christian literalism, I ask that you travel along with me a bit further to that juncture in the road where the religious and spiritual meet the political. Earlier I set out some Oxford Dictionary definitions of "liberal," "conservative," and "fundamentalist, which I repeat here for convenience:

Liberal: One who

>   ... is open-minded.

>   ... is not strict or rigorous, nor literal in making interpretations.

>   ... favors individual liberty and political and social reform.

>   ... regards many traditional beliefs as dispensable, invalidated by modern thought or liable to change.

Conservative: One who

>   ... tends to conserve.

>   ... is adverse to rapid change.

>   ... is moderate and avoids extremes.

>   ... allows only minor changes in traditional ritual, etc.

Fundamentalist: One who

>   ... strictly maintains traditional protestant beliefs such as the inerrancy of Scripture and literal acceptance of the creeds.

>   ... strictly maintains ancient and fundamental doctrines of any religion. I would add that fundamentalists regard such beliefs as absolute and give them supremacy over civil proclamations.

And just as night follows day, there are a number of political causes that can be associated with each of the three religious/spiritual perspectives:

Key public legislation or causes identified as "Liberal":

Social Security; Medicare; Civil Rights; suffrage (voting rights for women); equal rights for minorities, racial integration, and Affirmative Action; the right to choose (the "pro-choice" position on abortion); emphasis on all First Amendment (free speech) rights; protection of the environment; redistribution of wealth; and separation of Church and State. Can support such conservative causes such as fiscal discipline and declarations of war (World Wars I and II and the Vietnam War were undertaken by Democratic Presidents).[40]

Key public legislation or causes identified as "Conservative":

Fiscal discipline and supply side economics; a strong military; emphasis on the Second Amendment right to bear arms; a pro-business stance in regard to tax, social and environmental policies; and emphasis on Individual Responsibility vs. "the Welfare State." Can more easily support either certain liberal or fundamentalist causes.

Key public legislation or causes identified as "Fundamentalist":

State "support" of church ("We are a Christian nation") including prayer in public schools and favorable tax treatment; strong law enforcement; establishment of federal laws that would, for example, ban abortion and "gay" marriage; a strong military; and foreign policy influenced by a fundamentalist interpretation of the Bible including the "last days" or Armageddon, when a vengeful God—with Jesus on a white horse—slays all who are not Christian

---

[40] The intense part of the Vietnam War was under Democrat Lyndon Johnson from 1963-1968. then Republican Richard Nixon was elected and the intensity remained. It ended in 1975 after Republican Gerald Ford had become President.

fundamentalists. Can support conservative causes. (See the fundamentalist social agenda as described in Chapter Five.)

The definition of "liberal" does not distinguish between "liberal causes" (i.e., pro-choice, social security) and the way one holds a belief (open-mindedness versus closed-mindedness). Liberal extremists can be just as closed-minded as fundamentalist extremists. Likewise, a person can hold liberal, conservative or fundamentalist positions and be open-minded. Open-minded people welcome clarity and the making of distinctions.

How Lack Of Distinctions In Foreign Policy Costs Lives

At lunch yesterday at Miranda's (one of our very favorite restaurants) near Radda, an American turned to us and said, "Did you hear what's happening in Russia?" He was referring to the hostage crisis at the school in North Ossetia, which borders on Chechnya.

He went on to say something like "The terrorists have killed teachers. It's Al Qaeda."[41]

I responded, "I think not. You're speaking of the Chechens, aren't you? They are not Al Qaeda!"

"But," he says, "They are Muslims."

"Yes, the Chechnya Republic is Muslim. But they are not Al Qaeda. This *is* a terrible event, but it is not America's War on Terror."

Left unsaid (after all we were at lunch) was that Chechnya has been fighting for its independence since 1818! During the 20th

---

[41] Footnote for great-grandchildren: Al Qaeda is the name of a militant Muslim group led by Osama Bin Laden that flew planes into the World Trade Center on September 11, 2001. Like Bin Laden they were mostly from Saudi Arabia. They attacked the U.S. because of U.S. support for the Saudi leadership, which Al Qaeda wants to overthrow. By the time you (great grandchild) read this I believe it will be clear that Al Qaeda and Iraq were not working together (Bin Laden opposed the secular Muslim leadership of Saddam Hussein) and that the war on Iraq was a serious mistake for the United States. Despite the strong statement of the President's excellent non-partisan commission (5 Republicans and 5 Democrats) that there was no connection between Iraq and 9/11, 42% (Newsweek Poll on 10/22/04) of Americans still believed this. Our Vice President continues to make this claim, but this claim is unproven and not believed by any of our historic allies. Yet the President continues to infer such a connection.

century, Russia committed massive atrocities against hundreds of thousands of Chechens (think Stalin). The current struggle began in 1994. While the hostage crisis is despicable, so is the decade long destruction of the Chechnyan countryside and its capital city by the Russians.

The Russians have tanks and airplanes. The patriots (or insurgents or terrorists, depending on your political view) do not and must rely on other tactics. Is it more moral to bomb villages than to kill hostages?

Adding to the Chechnyan dilemma is the fact that many other former Soviet Republics are now independent—which, I predict, will eventually be the case for Chechnya. Further, the fact that the mostly—Muslim Chechnya is presently being ruled by Christian Russia adds fuel to the fire.

Prior to 2001, the United States was critical of Russia in this conflict. After 9/11 the U.S. agreed, in exchange for President Putin's support for our war on Al Qaeda (the perpetrators of the 9/11 tragedy) to call the Chechnyans "terrorists," instead of "freedom fighters." The Bush Administration has broadened the "war on terrorism" to include all groups fighting a legitimate government even though in the past the U.S. has supported the overthrow of elected governments (in Chili and Nicaragua). The Bush definition includes Palestinian groups such as Hamas and Hezbollah, the Chechnyans, the Basques of Spain, and the "insurgents" in Iraq which, like the others, were *not* involved in the 9/11 World Trade Center destruction. The Palestinians, like the Chechnyans, have been fighting for their own state—for independence, at least since 1948 when Israel was created, and many Palestinians lost their homes and land.

One fundamental disagreement about the so-called "War on Terrorism" is whether the enemy is Al Qaeda or *all* of these groups. The overwhelming European opinion is that Al Qaeda is the target, thus fueling huge disagreement with the American approach. Those who tend to see anti-American terrorism as primarily coming from Al Qaeda (think Bin Laden, World Trade Center 9/11) support the war in Afghanistan, where Al Qaeda was backed by the Taliban government. Most of the world overwhelmingly supports that effort. For example, at this writing, the French hold the NATO command in Afghanistan which was Germany's responsibility last year. That struggle is clearly targeted at Al Qaeda. In contrast, the war in Iraq is opposed by the overwhelming majority of nations, including some of our major traditional allies (the French, Canadian, Mexican and German governments, for example).

From the European view (and a view held by many conservative and liberal Americans) the war in Iraq and the war on terror are very different wars. It was Brent Scowcroft, National Security Advisor for George H. B. Bush (the father of our current President) who said recently, "Iraq is a serious and divisive diversion from the war on terror."[42]

Also referring to Iraq, Paul Weyrich, founder of the (conservative) Heritage Foundation said, "America is stuck in a guerrilla war with no end in sight… our real enemies… such as Al Qaeda, are benefiting from the Arab and Islamic backlash against our occupation of an Islamic country."[43]

Two very different words are used to describe those "guerrillas" fighting against established armies such as the U.S. (in Iraq) and Russia (in Chechnya). The word "insurgent" is defined (in the Oxford Dictionary) as one who rises in "active revolt, a rebel, revolutionary." The word "terrorist" is defined as a person who "uses or favors violent and intimidating methods of coercing a government." The word "insurgent" is used in Iraq because the fighters are mostly Baathists (Party of Saddam) Iraqis "rising in revolt" against the occupation and their loss of power. Insurgents are extremely difficult to defeat because they are from the local population and

---

[42] Brent Scowcroft, Former National Security Advisor for George W. Bush (the father).

[43] From "The Antiwar Right is Ready to Rumble," appearing in The New York Times on November 7, 2004.

are protected by their families and friends for many reasons including fear of retribution. The losses by the U.S. in Vietnam, Russia in Afghanistan and the French in Algeria are examples of how difficult it is to win against insurgents.

Terrorists, on the other hand, are usually foreigners and therefore easier to identify primarily because they are not well protected by the citizens, many of whom resent the terrorists' presence. It was easy for U.S. forces to defeat the Iraqi Army. But when the citizens got involved because of sentiment or intimidation, we found ourselves in an "insurgent" war—very difficult for an occupying army to win. Additionally, these insurgents often use "terrorist" methods in order to defeat a well-trained, well-equipped military force. Without condoning "terrorist" methods (or killing of innocent civilians by established armies) it is critical that we not label all groups who do acts of unconventional warfare as terrorists. Terrorists use terrorist methods. So, at times, do desperate people fighting for their freedoms or simply, protecting themselves. The U.S. itself has used terrorist methods in villages in Vietnam, in the current wars in Afghanistan and Iraq, against Native Americans and in countless other incidents in our history.

Further complicating the war in Chechnya (and U.S. policy in Iraq) are the distinctions Muslims themselves make about each other. For example, the Chechen fighters are *secular* Muslims. Al Qaeda would call them Infidels or non-believers. Al Qaeda holds the Chechen Muslins with the same disdain they have for Saudi Arabia or had for Saddam Hussein. To them, these secularists are Infidels!

Our American acquaintance in the restaurant is apparently unaware about the distinctions set out above. Those running the American government also either do not make such distinctions or do not acknowledge them. Their view is an example of "close-mindedness," where issues of peace and war are viewed with the kind of black-or-white simplicity that led us into the war in Vietnam and now provides the rationale for our presence in Iraq.

Had the American public opened its eyes—and minds, demanded clarity, and set aside its penchant for easy, black and white answers, probably neither the Viet Nam nor the Iraq war would have occurred. People die for lack of clarity and the misguided decisions that follow.[44] The planet cannot afford this kind of blindness.

A further word about the insurgent-as-"freedom-fighter" vs. "terrorist" debate. In Washington, since our invasion of Iraq, what were once the Chechnyan "freedom fighters" have now become "terrorists," not simply "insurgents." Chechnya is a territory—a republic by its government's definition. And the failure to consider terrorism as a tactic obscures the line between those who fight for their independence from oppressive rule and those whose aim is resistnace for ideological reasons.

Nations, such as Russia and Chechnya, can settle disputes by negotiating territory. While a truce in 1996 lasted for a few years, negotiations may now require the assistance of outsiders, but eventually, many predict, Chechnya will win either a high degree of autonomy or its independence. Likewise, the conflict between the Palestinians and the Israelis is between two national ("landed") movements. It goes back to 1917 and flourished after 1948. There was nearly a resolution in the 1990s. It is resolvable because territories can be negotiated.

Not so in the case of Al Qaeda. By contrast Al Qaeda is not a country but is, rather, a militant fundamentalist ideology, a loosely connected movement determined to overturn any Arab country

---

[44] Robert McNamara, Secretary of Defense during the escalation of the Vietnam War, has recently admitted to an amazing lack of clarity at his level about issues in Vietnam that are similar to those written about here. Oddly, as early as 1965 millions of Americans knew what he now knows. That administration did not distinguish between the civil war in the South (against the dictator the United States supported), the role of the North or that of China (an enemy of Vietnam for 1,000 years who we lumped together with Vietnam). We saw the world as black and white—free and communist—even though the communist nations differed greatly and the "free" world included many dictators. McNamara was a Democrat. The current administration is Republican. Does power corrupt? Does it blind leaders?

run by "Infidels" or non-believers, according to Bin Laden's definition. Ironically, Bin Laden wanted Saddam Hussein ousted. He succeeded with U.S. help. He also seeks to destroy the "Infidel" Western
influence in the world. The unresolved Palestinian issue feeds
recruits to his movement as has the U.S. invasion of Iraq, which is
why the British Ambassador to Italy created few rebuttals in Europe
in mid-September (2004) with his statement that President George
W. Bush is Al Qaeda's "best recruiter." In this view, the U.S. is seen
as having diverted military and intelligence resources away from Al
Qaeda while encouraging recruits for them.

Porter Goss, the new CIA Director, in early 2005 told the
Senate Intelligence Committee, "Islamic extremists are exploiting
the Iraqi conflict to recruit new anti-U.S. jihadists…(who will) leave
Iraq experienced and focus on acts of urban terrorism,"

Al Qaeda was supported and encouraged by the Taliban
Muslim fundamentalist government in Afghanistan. The world-wide
support for that war (in sharp contrast with the U.S. invasion of Iraq)
is demonstrated by NATO support. Without a national base, however, it is harder to target Al Qaeda, which is a loosely knit world-wide
movement. It has no territory to negotiate. Thus it is infinitely more
difficult to fight Al Qaeda because it is not a "place" (who do we
bomb, for example?) with borders to negotiate, like the Chechnyan
and Israeli–Palestinian disputes, and because it is an ideology.

The positions that have guided U.S. policy and opposing positions which I am describing here are difficult to "prove." Rather, they
are statements of belief. Though not given as the original reason for
the invasion of Iraq (original reasons such as the presence of
weapons of mass destruction and ties to Al Qaeda have both been
discredited), President Bush now speaks of the "transformational
power of liberty" as the reason for the war. The theory is that turning Iraq into a democracy will transform the Middle East. If we suc-
ceed in this, the results of Bush's "vision" could be very positive. But

achieving this result will be exceedingly difficult in a country where tribal loyalties remain strong. The January 2005 Iraqi election and the proud symbol of the "purple finger" of those who voted seem to be positive signs. Future generations would surely celebrate such an achievement.

But, in the meantime, you and I, my American acquaintance in the restaurant, and certainly our government leaders must begin to make clear distinctions, that is, as clear as humans can.

Will The American "Empire" Decline?

Of course. That's what empires do after a while. And such declines, if we can judge by history, are hastened by hubris[45], by going it alone, by insisting it must be "my way or the highway." A word used in Europe to describe America in 2004 was "bully," referring to the way many allies felt treated by the U.S.

Historically, empires develop a class structure to support the nobles whose job it is to protect the peasants. The nobles get wealthy, and the peasants fight the wars, at least a bit similar to what is happening in the U.S. today. True, while the rich-poor gap is increasing, mobility, though decreasing, is still possible. Emperors stay in power by fomenting a state of war, reminding people of the danger from "the other guys," and promising to provide security. Sound familiar?

But we would decline even if these things weren't true. The American intention was not to be an "Empire" but it has become an awesome power. It is the nature of empires and of power to decline. It's easy to remember this in Tuscany. The Roman Empire was finished 1500 years ago. So in this amazing place with Roman remains there is no great military power.

At a wine shop in Radda today, John talked about the continuing strong influence of paganism in Italy. Paganism, or peasant religion, reflects the sacredness of all creation. The sacredness also

---

45 Overweening pride

means the deep connection with the soil, the elements, the grapes and olives—with life—*vita!*

John, an American-born Irishman, many years ago chose Tuscany as his place. He didn't choose a government or an empire; he chose the land. It is one thing to love one's country and protect it. I believe that it is a better thing to love one's *land* and the life one has created upon it.

When I heard John speak of his life here in Tuscany, I thought of the Joseph Campbell statement, "The world is a mess. It has always been a mess." And then he urges us to find our own self or, in his words, "Follow your bliss!"

Our host, Giuliano Tofanelli at Palazzo di Luglio in Sansepolcro, took extreme pride in the archway he had built under which he served us figs hand-picked from the tree within our view, just outside the dining room door. He proudly served the olive oil harvested from the olive trees also within our sight and pressed by his own hand, and after a dusting of salt, he poured it tenderly on our Tuscan bread–a celebration of life!

The end of the empire?[46] I don't worry too much about it. We can't prevent it. Better we should put our own life in order and perhaps "the best is yet to be."

It looks that way today, writing this amidst the Tuscan hills.

What About School Prayer?

> "In God we trust" on the coins.
>
> "Under God" in our Pledge of Allegiance.
>
> "Ten Commandments" on public property.
>
> "Prayer in Schools."

To Christian literalists, these demonstrations of a closer link between church and state are hopeful signs in an increasingly secular culture. Perhaps history suggests some parallels.

---

[46] This assumes that the U.S. is an empire. Probably it is not, if judged by land conquered and the length of dominance. Perhaps, more accurately, it is simply an awesome military, political and economic power.

The decline of the Roman Empire coincided with the rise of Christian power in Rome. Constantine declared Rome Christian in 312 A.D. thus uniting Christianity with the most powerful military of that time, which was afterwards used in the "service of Jesus". The emperor pointed to a higher power to justify his conquest. My ancestors were "converted" to Christianity by the Roman sword.

Two centuries later, the Roman Empire was gone.

When spirituality declines, politicians (in church and state) attempt to get the right words said, as if saying "Under God" means it is so. In the United States to win elections, candidates speak the word "God" frequently. "God Bless America" is a campaign mantra.

How different this is from early America. "Our constitution never mentions a deity aside from the pro forma phrase 'in the year of our Lord.'" When Ben Franklin suggested a prayer, "Alexander Hamilton argued that if people knew that the delegates were resorting to prayer it would be seen as an act of desperation."[47] George Washington and many other founding Fathers were deists—that is, *not* theists or Trinitarians (God the Father, Son, and Holy Spirit)[48]. They were passionate about the separation of church and state.

The school prayer issue illustrates the absurdity of the current American situation. The New York State Board of Regents wrote a prayer and imposed it on all students and teachers as a daily practice. The U.S. Supreme Court said "no" to this practice. Individuals can pray, but the Court, speaking about the "Regent's Prayer" stated that state (government) cannot impose their prayer on all students and teachers. And who would want such an imposition?

Worse, in the conflicts about prayer in schools how much clarity is there about what the Supreme Court said "no" to? Reactive emotionality is powerful. Too often it trumps clarity and true spirituality.

---

[47] Both quotes are from an article by Kenneth C. Davis entitled "Jefferson, Madison, Newdow?" appearing in The New York Times on March 26, 2004.

[48] The Deists believed that God simply set the universe in motion but has no continuing involvement in it and that belief in the existence of God is not based on supernatural inspiration but rather is the result of logical reasoning and observation of nature (more specifically, it mirrors a universe based on the theories of Newton). Theism, however, does not exclude revelation as the basis of a belief in God.

What About Abortion?

As I write, abortion is a huge issue in the United States. While elsewhere I claim labels are too simple and misleading, I will use them here to better describe the debate over this issue.

Liberals and Conservatives both want to reduce the number of abortions—legal and illegal. But they have different approaches to accomplishing this. Liberals point to countries like Belgium and the Netherlands where abortions are legal and excellent services are available to pregnant women. These two countries have the lowest abortion rates in the world. Their philosophy is that if you oppose abortion and especially the consequences of illegal abortions, then legalize it. This guarantees that abortions will be done safely, and, only after good family planning services, help women make more rational choices both before pregnancy and after.

In the U.S., all abortions stayed stable during the Reagan years when federally-funded services were curtailed in the U.S. and decreased 11% during the Clinton years when more services were again available.

Similar results are found in statistics on abortions provided to unmarried women. During the Reagan and Bush years (1980-1992), the increase was over 11%, the largest gain ever for the post-Roe vs. Wade period (1973 when abortion was legalized). During the Clinton years, the gain was 3% and less than 1% during his last five years in office.

The rate rose at nearly the same pace in the Nixon, Ford, Carter and Reagan years.[49] According to Nicholas Kristof, abortions, "…have increased significantly during President Bush's presidency."[50]

Of course, there are many variables that affect such statistics. However, it appears that when people (both males and females) are educated to examine choices, understand clear consequences about whether to engage in sexual activities or abstain from them, and

---

[49] The source for this information is the National Center for Health Statistics as quoted in an Associate Press story run in the Seattle Times on November 26, 2004.

[50] New York Times, March 16, 2005. Recent studies suggest otherwise. (See Mike Stobbe, Assiociated Press, December 20, 2005, Seattle Post-Intelligencer.)

whether to use contraceptives or not, births out of wedlock, sexually transmitted diseases, and abortions decrease.

Despite such research across the decades, most conservatives favor a ban on legal abortions except in most extreme cases (pregnancies resulting from rape or termination to save the life of the mother, for instance). They eliminate or under-fund federally-supported services to women believing that such services encourage more abortions. Money is pulled out of national and international programs for women when conservatives are in power in Washington because they believe that "abortion counseling" may be part of the offerings. Fundamentalists, however, go a step further, demanding a Constitutional amendment to ban abortion in the U.S.

These examples suggest that liberals, conservatives and fundamentalists take very different positions. Which do you favor? I believe that abortion is essentially a medical and family issue to be decided by the pregnant mother after consultation.

Which leads to a central question: When does life begin? What the right-to-life believers offer us is an arbitrary determination (though they believe it) that life begins at conception. Another popular and also, arbitrary opinion is that life begins at birth (consciousness). Nobody knows. Nobody sees a soul[51] enter at conception.

What About Gay Marriage?

Religious organizations are free to make their own rules about marriage, divorce, contraception, adultery, masturbation, and so forth. They are free to enforce or not enforce these rules.

But marriage is also a civil contract accompanied by various laws that govern its recognition and dissolution. When the state issues a marriage license, it is issued to those who have reached legal maturity (adult status) which in most states occurs at age 18. At the present, most states further specify that the contract be between

---

[51] A Greek concept separating body from soul. Hebrews saw the person as a whole being, not divided.

only two people (polygamy is thus illegal). And that's it. So if gays—two people of the same sex who have reached maturity—want to marry (or civilly unite), of course they should receive the legal recognition of the state. However, if they want their legal union blessed by a church or other religious body, then they would naturally need to meet the rules and requirements of that body.

Church and state—separate domains that I believe should remain separate. In a theocracy the church determines both church and civil law. In a democracy civil law is separate. Civil authorities do not require any church to recognize same-sex civil marriage (or "civil union") of opposite sex marriages or "common-law" arrangements. Similarly, in a democracy, the church cannot declare that the marriage between people of the same sex is illegal, but it may declare it to be immoral and ban its sacramental recognition.

When we look at the statistics, we see that heterosexual marriage is struggling. Roughly 50% end up in divorce. It is utter nonsense to believe that the greatest threat to heterosexual marriage is the prospect of homosexual marriages, as many fundamentalists in the U.S. claim. All of us should be pleased that anyone wants to make such a profound commitment.

Actually, 60% of Americans support either gay marriage or civil unions. Citizens supporting civil law should be pleased that gays (who vote, pay taxes and die in wars) also are granted the equal economic, medical and inheritance privileges that come to those who are married as well as the opportunity for spiritual growth that the marital commitment may bring.

If fundamentalists want to "protect" marriage they should literally obey the Bible. For example, Jesus *never* refers to sexual orientation. The idea of sexual "orientation" is a modern concept. The word "homosexual" entered the English language only about 100 years ago. The Bible (Leviticus 20:13) condemns what we now call homosexuality with the same ferocity (death) that it condemns working on the Sabbath or being a wizard and many other acts. There is no record of anyone receiving this penalty. The Greeks considered homosexuality to be normal behavior. Throughout history people have adopted various sexual practices but did not think in terms like "gay," "straight," or "bi-sexual." Certainly the Bible makes no reference to gay marriage.

There is much in the Bible about protecting marriage. Focusing on those passages is probably more useful than worrying about gay marriage as a "threat to the family." Since one of the Ten Commandments very clearly states, "Thou shalt not commit adultery," how can anyone doubt that the Bible and church support marriage?

But how about a Constitutional amendment forbidding divorce and adultery? After all, many Mideastern countries list adultery as a crime. The churches seem to be helpless to stem the tide of adultery and divorce among their own married (and divorced) constituents. So perhaps we need a civil law to fix the situation and adequate funding to enforce it.

Absurd? Of course! An amendment to the Constitution to take away rights! That's exactly what's been proposed by fundamentalist Christians regarding the issue of gay marriage. Opposing gay marriage is a "moral value" to some and bigotry to others. But let the *law* stop at limits of age (18) and let the church worry about gender.

Some additional statistics about the issue: Roughly five to 10% of humans born are gay and 50-60% are straight. The other 30-40% are somewhere in between (bi-sexual). It's a continuum from very, very gay to very, very straight.

That's the way it is.

Roughly five to 10% of our GIs in World War II were gay. That translates into from thirty to fifty thousand gays who died as U.S. soldiers, let alone thousands of Russian, French, British, Japanese, German, Italian, and Chinese gays who died defending their country. Hitler killed an estimated half-million suspected gays in his camps. This very fact should be instructive to those who oppose civil rights for gays.

Gays have contributed mightily to our culture. Where would we be without Walt Whitman, Leonardo da Vinci, Michelangelo, Tchaikovsky, King James I (the guy behind the King James Bible), Alexander the Great, Cole Porter, Rock Hudson, Sappho (600 B.C.—the first romantic poet), Socrates, Plato, Richard the Lion Hearted, Julius III (1487-1555—Catholic Pope), Christina (1626-1689—Swedish Queen), Peter the Great, Frederick the Great, Hans Christian Andersen, Chief Crazy Horse, Gertrude Stein, Bessie Smith (1894-1937—African-American Blues Singer), Virginia Woolf, T.E. Lawrence (Lawrence of Arabia), James Baldwin, Tennessee Williams, Billie Jean King, Frieda Kahlo, Elton John, Ellen Degeneres, Melissa Etheridge? The list is endless and includes millions of men and women across the planet.

Finally, what about this claim that gay orientation is a choice? Sexuality a choice? Not for me. I can still name three of the girls I fell in love with from first grade to fourth grade. Are you kidding me—a choice? As a little boy (ages one to seven) I was deeply bonded to my same age cousin Milton, and close to his older brother Earl, who lived three houses away. I was very fond of other male friends during these young years, but I never gave them a Shirley Temple ring which was a big deal in 1936. Only Nancy, my first-grade love, with whom I rarely talked, got this expensive five-cent ring. However, I have male (gay) friends who fell in love in first grade with boys!

An Associated Press article (February 19, 2005) by Lauren Neergaard calls attention to the fact that "roughly one in 4,000 babies are born with both male and female traits." In these babies you cannot tell gender by looking at genitals. Since the gender is unclear by viewing, factors such as chromosomes (female XX, male XY) and sex hormones have been used to decide. But there are other factors such as a genetic hard-wiring in the brain before birth that is unmeasurable and can only be understood when the child at age 4 1/2 and up finally pronounces "I'm a boy! And picks a boy's name!"

Since surgery has been a frequent past practice immediately after birth this greatly complicates the child's life when he or she begins to believe that the sex chosen by the surgeon (and parents) at birth doesn't fit!

"…and more doctors are putting off sex assignment surgery… then if at age 12 they say, 'No, I'm a girl,' at least you haven't damaged anything…"

One in 4,000. Do the math. That means in the U.S. 75,000 citizens were born with no clear genital gender identity. In the world that's 1,500,000.

Given this gender confusion why is it so difficult to understand that sexual orientation is probably hard-wired in the brain? Almost all homosexuals have grown up with heterosexual parents. Recent evidence supports that growing up with gay parents has no impact on one's orientation.

Here's my idea about those who believe the "choice" theory. People who are bi-sexual and who therefore can be attracted to either sex are the ones most capable of making those choices and the ones who often think that everyone else has the same interest. But I would ask those in this particular group of people not to project that capability (gift) onto the rest of us who are decidedly in one camp or the other! For most of us, it is simply not a choice. It is a discovery made difficult in a homophobic society.

What About Inter-Racial Marriage?

Isn't the phrase "inter-racial marriage" an oxymoron? If we all came out of Africa, there are no separate "races." Are you light-skinned? Your ancestors must have journeyed north and needed lighter skin to take in more sun (think of those dark winter nights in Norway). Of course, there are tribal and ethnic differences. There are also ethnic and religious differences. And we have people of many nationalities on the earth. Too often, however, these differences come to divide us, when it should be clear—and more important—what unites us: we are all one.

What About Underlying Values?

In all the issues above, there is, at the core of each, a set of values that informs whatever political position one chooses. School prayer? Abortion? Gay marriage? War? Tell me your position, and I'll tell you what values you hold. Values are principles that are important to you. Unfortunately, one person's values may be seen by another as bigoted or cruel or un-Christian.

Slavery was a strongly held "value" across the world for thousands of years. The Christian church in America defended slavery as "Biblical." In I Peter 2:18,[52] we find: "Servants [translated as "slaves" in modern versions), be subject to your masters with all fear; not only to the good and gentle, but also to the froward." (I quoted this 1611 King James Version because it was the version likely used in the 17th, 18th and 19th century even though its use of old "Shakespearian" English may be confusing. For instance, the word "froward" means "perverse; difficult to deal with.") Slavery was practiced in the U.S., at least legally, until it was prohibited by the 13th Amendment to the Constitution on December 6, 1865.

So the practice of slavery represents a value and anti-slavery represents a different value. Similarly, favoring of gay rights represents a value and so does the opposing view. A pro-choice position on abortion represents a value, and opposing choice, that is, imposing a legal ban on abortion, also represents a value.

When my political views are different from yours, it usually means that my values are different from yours but that doesn't make *your* values *not* values. It simply makes them different from mine.

---

[52] Also see Ephesians 6:5; Colossians 3:22; Titus 2:9 and Deuteronomy 12:12 in the Hebrew scriptures where slavery is taken for granted by God!

"In '*New Seeds of Contemplation*,' Trappist monk Thomas Merton warns of the danger of a theology that exaggerates distinctions between this and that, good and evil, right and wrong. 'These distinctions become irreducible divisions. No longer is there any sense that we might perhaps all be more or less at fault, and that we might be expected to take upon our own shoulders the wrongs of others by forgiveness, acceptance, patient understanding and love, and thus help one another to find truth. On the contrary, in [this] theology, the important thing is to be absolutely right and to prove that everybody else is absolutely wrong.' He calls this a theology of the devil."[53]

If I, in any way in this book, have encouraged a "my way is right, yours is wrong" attitude, forgive me. Rather I would encourage compassion and not contempt for differing views. To quote Rumi, the 13th century Islamic mystic, "Out beyond the place of doing right and doing wrong there is a field…I will meet you there."

America is in a crisis about values. We have to face that crisis not in a self-righteous way but with respect for differing values and differing resulting political views, looking for commonalities on which to build dialogue. For instance, almost everyone wants to reduce abortion. Almost everyone wants to stop killing. Almost everyone wants to reduce teenage pregnancy and drug use.

As I do my last editing I see the values confusion further evidenced by current events and the emphasis placed on Terri Schiavo, the woman who has lived by a feeding tube for 15 years, versus the lack of a public outcry and national familiarity and emotion about the following:

> …the genocide and displacement (almost two million have fled their homes) in Sudan

> … the people denied due process, stripped, beaten and in 26 cases killed by U.S. troops.

---

[53] "Beyond who's right, wrong" by Lalor Cadley. The Atlanta Journal-Constitution. March 5, 2005

... the Jose Medellin case (attracting world attention) where he as a Mexican was apparently denied legal help in violation of a U.S. treaty.[54]

... the ongoing tragedy in the Congo which has been described as equal to ... "having a tsunami every month for the last six years."

... the nearly 5000 Iraqi citizens (mostly children) kidnapped in the last year and a half, as well as the thousands killed since the U.S. invasion.

... the billions of dollars in proposed cuts in Medicare which will certainly affect the poor.

All of these together have not received the press coverage of the Schiavo case, not to mention the Michael Jackson trial. Are the others simply too much to handle: Are we immune from those sufferings or are they too painful and too removed from our day to day existence?

Would Shakespeare's Hamlet say again now, "The time is out of joint. Oh cursed spite that ever I was born to get it right?

No one has a corner on "the good" values, and all of us have a huge stake in identifying our commonalities and finding compromise. Since the Bible can be used to defend liberal or fundamentalist "values," it doesn't make sense to claim that my values are "right" because they're based on the Bible (or yours are "wrong" because they're not). Instead, we can both benefit by following this simple exhortation from the Hebrew Scriptures: "Come now and let us reason together." Isaiah 1:18.

---

[54] Associated Press, "Death Penalty Case gets World Notice" by Hope Yen, March 29, 2005.

Part Three:
The Spiritual Road Beyond Literalism

Caffé Bar-Ucci

CHAPTER TEN: CORE MORALITIES

So, what is a core morality? Paraphrasing Ross Snyder[55], "It is a call to meaningful living, a way to *be* rather than a list of prohibitions or admonitions. As such, it is forever dynamic, enticing each of us to discover deeper and deeper layers of meaning." Thus, it leads us to a new mythos that helps to harmonize our purposes and behaviors.

I notice my hesitancy to write further. The very act of listing these attributes of core moralities has its frightening side for me. I recall vividly a certain youth who had been raised a strict Catholic. In 1970, I had come to know him as a true-believer hippie celebrating his religious rites with drugs and preaching the virtues thereof. Later I knew him as a fundamentalist Christian. He believed that he had changed in these three manifestations, but it seemed to me that nothing basic had changed. The dependent child seeking a true belief had simply changed hats. My fear is that this same man would accept the core moralities as a new dogma rather than as the challenges they are. The drive to "know-for-sure what I know" is still overwhelming to many.

Going beyond that fear, I offer a compilation of core principles, grouped under four different headings in this chapter, and begin with one that has special meaning for me: graceful aging.

1. The Core Morality of Graceful Aging

When a three-year-old looks at an eight-year-old s/he sees a big and old person. At eight years one can hardly imagine being 18, and so it goes. All of us are aging.

---

[55] Ross Snyder, who developed the phrase "core morality," taught at the Chicago Theological Seminary from 1941 until about 1977. He represents a style of teaching that celebrates education as an event more than as a passing of knowledge. For him, teacher and student are two humans exploring meaning together. To quote him freely, "Life is meant to be lived. All of us are meant to be participants, not merely spectators. Organizing a life-world and taking it some place is what life is all about. It is the goal that includes all other goals."

Many cultures venerate youth. This doesn't make sense because all of the venerators are getting older. Even idolized youth are getting older. Isn't it ridiculous to venerate that which nobody is becoming? Isn't it much more sensible to venerate the inevitable—becoming older? To place supreme value on youth is life-denying, for it implies that we are better at the beginning of life than at the end, and that the physical vitality when young trumps the possible wisdom one gains in the aging process.

Many have a tragic view of this aging process. Many have accepted the idea that getting old is a matter of having less of everything—fun, sexual pleasure, and brainpower. As a result, many people choose to fulfill such unhappy prophecies, although none of them is a necessary consequence of aging. They have decided to believe that such tribulations are inevitable. In contrast to this insanity, I propose that we live life in such a way that those younger will say, "How wonderful it must be to be your age."

It is obviously true that aged persons have a higher susceptibility to some diseases than younger persons. And, of course, it is in old age that anyone who has lived a healthy, fulfilling life will die. And before that the body slows down. That's what is! It need not be my primary definition of myself. One's well-being has less to do with age than with such things as how healthy one's body is, how one feels about one's appearance or whether one likes oneself. Do you project openness to others? How does your view of life get communicated to others? Are you optimistic, spirited, curious, risk-taking, playful? How genuine is your sense of humor? How willing are you to learn? These characteristics we admire can be manifested at any age.

There are many ways to resist what might be called the conspiracy against learning how to grow older in our culture. One way is to study worn-out, older people and consciously decide not to be like them—that is, acting as if you were losing your value, wearing out, and dying. That kind of aging is a role that is learned; it is not only influenced by many forces in our culture, but it is finally a personal decision each of us makes. Some people seem to think, "I'm old so I have to act old, think old." In contrast, the key to good mental and physical health is the ability to remain alert. How joyous it is to meet the many elderly people who face the vicissitudes of the aging process and remain fully alive.

So each of us should ask—regardless of age—what message are we giving the world about growing older. If you're 23, what message are you sending 13-year-olds and eight-year-olds? If you're 47, what is your life saying about aging? Do younger persons rejoice that you are so alive, whatever your age? Graceful aging is a way of venerating being alive, of seeing purpose in the whole of life—and saying no to the stereotypes that lead to senility and premature death.

I cringe when I hear someone tell a teenager, "Enjoy it, the teens are the best years." I feel sad for the speaker. Those beyond their teens have had many more years to experience the joy of being. All of us are getting older. Why not look forward to it? Why not create the future we want rather than lament that we are not what we used to be? "Do not let death find you already a corpse. Let him find you in full dance," says the sage. My wish for you: May you be so blessed as to live long enough to experience the aches and pains of aging and the peace and joy that comes to those who use life's experiences to gain wisdom and to understand the essential simplicity of it all.

2. The Core Morality Of Striving For Authenticity

Notice that Ross Snyder did not call this a morality *of* authenticity but rather one of *striving* for authenticity. It is not a mountaintop we someday reach. It is a journey.

Snyder did his writing in the context of adults coming clean with youth. He focuses on the phoniness in the older ones when they pretend to know more than they know, be who they are not, or deny the errors and inadequacies that are part of being human, younger or older.

Being authentic is knowing what you care about and standing up for that. It is being in touch with and "owning" your emotional states: fear, hope, joy, anger, love, hate, sadness, whatever. It is being aware of your defensiveness and acknowledging it and choosing to defend or not defend your ego-self. It is the ability to accept either not knowing and the resulting feelings of inadequacy, or knowing and feelings of confidence and success as life twists and turns.

Think for a moment about someone dear to you. Get this person clearly in mind. Now, ask how much that person knows about your fears, your hurts, your pain. How well does that person know the real you? Would that person be surprised to know that when asked to focus on someone special while reading this, you picked him/her? Does that person know how central s/he is for you? Does that person know about your concerns, especially in relation to that person's life and welfare? If you fear that s/he will go away, does that person know about that fear? If your answer is "no" to these questions, then your authentic self is not known to this person.

Many readers of this book who are in their fifties or older grew up in an age when politeness and thinking of the other first was the norm. They were told, "Don't offend anybody." However, few mentioned that if you make that your life's cornerstone, you will never experience the *depth* of love. Pain and joy are partners just as love and hate are forever joined. Both exist together. They are not opposites. When hate and pain are treated as if they were the enemy of love and joy, the fear is that there will be no relationship. The opposite of love/hate, which are horns on the same goat, are indifference and apathy. Authenticity embraces both the valleys and the mountains of life.

Ruth Emory[56] has written that "The authentic individual will not pretend to stand on ground which is not in reality his/her ground ... . This is really you, and not a 'put on' person. Authentic life means that people can feel able to trust you because they know you mean what you say and really are as you seem. There is an assurance that even though they may hate what you are and stand for, they can depend on it. You are no will-o-the-wisp."

She adds these ways in which this core morality may be expressed:

> Individuals are fully aware of their possibilities as well as their limitations, and are not denying them. They are able to say that they do not know something and not be frightened by the necessity for such acknowledgment. They invite a critical scrutiny of their ideas and really welcome what comes without either supinely acquiescing or loudly defending. They expect others to be authentic and they help them discover who they are and where they live, and are sensitive to—but not 'thrown' by—their inconsistencies as they find their personhood. They are open and able to receive messages about themselves without becoming unduly hostile or resentful. They give their whole being to a group, come with all they are—and do not hold anything back since it is important to be as honest as possible. They say what they truly believe to be the case insofar as they can see it, and not what they think they are expected to say; but they also speak responsibly, not out of whim or smallness of spirit.

Such authenticity begins with self-differentiation. Before I can be authentic, of course, I must know who I am; I must distinguish between me and my history, between my ego-self and my real

---

56 Ruth Emory was Snyder's student from 1957 to 1959. A powerful teacher in her own right, she credits him with inspiring concepts that continue to enlighten her everyday experience. She, Rene Pino and I developed training for youth workers in the Methodist Church in the 1960's with these concepts as guides.

self. I must accept that experience is not external to self but *continuously created within*[57]. Only then will I speak for myself and not believe that what I am experiencing is what all are or should be experiencing. My reality is not your reality. With such clarity I may avoid believing that my feelings are "our" feelings, my thoughts, "our" thoughts, my perceptions "our" perceptions, my reality "our" reality! Authentic behavior is grounded in such differentiation.

Striving for authenticity reduces the pretending, game-playing way of being in the world. It opens the door for intimacy in relationships, for integrity in the marketplace, and for openness among people of differing backgrounds.

3. The Core Morality Of Commitment

Commitment is the glue that holds together all other core moralities and, more importantly, holds together humans, the social fabric, and the web of life that encompasses all life forms. Commitment, not methods, is what drives humans. My commitment to a certain core morality is the spark and the flame. Methods and strategies may fail, but if committed, I continue toward my vision.

I list two major areas of commitment: commitment to relationships and commitment to community values.

Commitment to Relationships

Intimacy, trust, and openness require that my commitment to others transcend the particular agenda I might have for them and the particular feelings which I may have at the moment. For instance, if I am angry at you this does not mean my commitment to our relationship will end. The message "You can count on me" means I am committed to caring for someone—regardless of my own troubles. Further, it means I am committed to your growth and your choices.

---

[57] This statement is inspired by Dr. Ron Short. (See Bibliography)

Midwifery as a Way of Being

This means that my commitment is to "be" in such a way as to assist others in their birthing of ideas, plans for actions, dreams, self-definitions, and core moralities. Snyder applied the world "midwifery" to such assisting. Ruth Emory describes it this way:

> To midwife means to assist at birth. To assist is really all that can be done—to help this idea come forth; to encourage a person to take that position; to help someone find courage to come to terms with him/herself.... Midwifery does not dictate the outcome. It helps what is there to be born.... Midwifery [does not mean] trying to dictate the results of the birthing process [but rather] to offer a bulwark of strength and support and a safe place of refuge during the working out of feelings and while frail images are being examined and understood."

It is surely clear to any midwife assisting in the birth of a newborn that the child is not hers. It is not so clear in the kind of midwifery to which I am referring. In those areas about which we feel passionate, an inherent tension exists between the desire to midwife and the desire to dictate the results. The growing edge in this core morality is the struggle between those poles.

Parents—No Matter What!

Of course, parents attempt to dictate or at least shape the growing-up process of their children, which is to be expected of those responsible for raising a decent human being. But what makes this fatal in parenting is when the parent withdraws all love and support when the child "makes the wrong choice." They fail to make the kind of commitment to their children that says, "We will be here for you through your growing-up years." Instead, too many parents say, in effect, that "our commitment to you is dependent on your behavior and whether your beliefs reflect ours." One study conducted in Seattle, for example, indicated that 40 percent of homeless teens were homosexual or bisexual. American society pays a heavy price for homophobia and the parental rejection of youth because of their sexual orientation. This is just one example of behavior that will seriously undermine parental support and involvement in a child's life.

"To be a parent," says Snyder, "means to be a faithful friend of the growth of a son or daughter—come hell or high water." And any of us who have parented our kids through adolescence know that on some days it rains pretty hard and the water rises: we are angry, disappointed, frustrated, sad, hurt. But our commitment to these aliens-in-residence, who once were our adorable five-year-olds, remains. No matter what.

Love, Marriage and Partnership

Nowhere is this need for commitment more vivid than in relationships with our partners. Falling in love is wonderful. It's an emotion. Romance is an emotion. But emotions do not sustain a relationship. Sustaining requires a commitment. Commitment is a *choice*, not a *feeling*. It is a commitment to bond. For those denied the right to marry, partnership also can contain that commitment.

Emotions come and go. They are a natural part of life. Romance comes and goes. So how, in even the most committed relationships, do we renew romance? First, one must be honest about differences, disappointments and misunderstandings, anger and frustration. "Absence makes the heart grow fonder" is, literally, about physical absence but it is, essentially and spiritually, allowing oneself to experience those many moments in a relationship when something's amiss. Hurt feelings, anger, stonewalling silence, raised voices, moments of misunderstanding that can seem to threaten the relationship offer an opportunity to rekindle romance through honest dialogue. When the emotional honeymoon ends, what must take its place are commitment and the skills to "hang in" and deal openly with difficulties.

So, second, there are skills to be learned; ways of communicating with each other, of listening to each other, of owning up to one's behavior toward the other. When you say "I'm angry" to your partner, it defines that moment and that moment only. Nothing else. It does not mean "You're bad." If it means anything more than this-is-what-I-feel-here-and-now-in-this-moment, it is that you trust me enough to tell me about your internal reaction. The same with "I hate you," the twin of "I love you." (The opposite of both is indifference!)

Third, there's the fact that each party to the relationship likely had different secondhand learnings about conflict or differences and how to handle them. Since opposites attract, likely one is talkative and the other quiet, one takes command and the other acquiesces, one thinks it through carefully and the other "leaps before looking," one is quick with anger and the other quick with a smile that says, "Let's forget it." (This is why learning good communication and listening skills is important.)

The commitment to bond is a profound act of love. It includes the commitment to get whatever help is needed to transcend childhood second-hand learnings that are damaging your relationships. The hope is to learn some new "how to deal with difference" skills so that romance again and again can be renewed. A good therapist can teach these things and provide help.

Love is passion.

Love is friendship—brotherly or sisterly love.

Love is bonding/a choice.

Love is spiritual—"love your enemies as yourself."

Love may be sensual/sexual, but sex without compassion is simply a physiological experience—not love.

Love is romance.

Love as romance is what the troubadours of the medieval years were about. They separated romance from marriage and sex. Marriages were arranged. Couples grew to "love" each other, hopefully, over the years

Since the word "love" has many differing meanings it is not simple to sort out what's meant with each usage. For the troubadours, romance was enflamed by longings that were not "fulfilled" in sex or marriage. For them, romance was its own beautiful experience. The great love stories of the middle ages—Romeo and Juliet, Tristan and Isolde, Abelard and Heloise—are all tales of such romance. Even today, our love stories (think country music) tell us that "forbidden" love conquers. When romance or "falling in love" is fulfilled then one moves to a new stage in the relationship where romance comes and goes depending on how the relationship is handled.

I know about romantic feelings. From first grade on I remember girls and later women I "fell in love" with. Now, every morning I sit here at Bar-Ucci in Chianti writing. Patricia will drive up the hill at about noon. She will park the car in the lot unseen from here. At a certain moment I will look up and see her. No matter where I am in my writing I will stop—my heart will be filled with happiness, and I will experience again—enhanced by her smile as she catches my glance—the romantic tug at the same place in my heart that I remember (if any of us can truly remember such moments) as a boy in love. But now it is enriched by our 27-year-old relationship, our 18-year marriage, and for me, by my lifetime spiritual journey.

Deep partnership is a bonding requiring profound commitment. At its core, it is sustained by choice, not feelings. Bonding love is a choice to journey together, transcending feelings of love and hate, romance or disdain. Feelings will come and go. Romance will come and go. Emotionality cannot be the primary criterion by which the success of bonding is measured. Deep partnership is grounded in commitment. We are in it together, no matter what.

> I want a partner
>
> With whom I can dance
>
> Who does not ask of me
>
> Or us
>
> Or life
>
> Too much of what it cannot bring.

Commitment to Community Values

As marriages fail and families splinter, we hear more and more about the need for community. For me, this means a commitment to a certain set of values.

Inclusiveness—Count Me In!

This is the era of support groups, and for good reason. We all need to live out our lives at least striving to help build communities of significance. Over the centuries, many religious people have hoped that their religious institution was such a community. On occasion it has been, and often it has not been. In our times, common-interest groups such as alcoholics, gays, women, senior citizens, parents without partners, and minorities have actively developed support communities. These groups often have a powerful positive influence.

For support communities to avoid narrowness, however, I encourage a diversity sometimes not found in a single-interest approach. It is unwise to continuously segregate people by age or by any other characteristic. For example, a teen, experiencing the pitfalls of life, may find a sixty-year-old who knows how to be a friend. Married and single people need to learn how to be together. Men and women need to be together. Gays and straights and teens and elders need to be together. Indeed, in more *inclusive* communities the search for values is most likely to be sharpened as imagined or real differences are confronted.

JUSTICE: FIRST THE NAZIS CAME . .

First the Nazis came...

First they came for the communists, and I did not speak out—because I was not a communist;

Then they came for the socialists, and I did not speak out—because I was not a socialist;

Then they came for the trade unionists, and I did not speak out—because I was not a trade unionist;

Then they came for the Jews, and I did not speak out—because I was not a Jew;

Then they came for me—and there was no one left to speak out for me. [58]

These words come from the horrors of the Holocaust and were voiced again in the struggle against apartheid in Africa and for civil rights in the South. Especially in the light of recent civil rights violations by our own government, we must routinely ask ourselves such questions, as does Ross Snyder in the following:

Where will I stand and fight for others? How do I overcome the evil I meet? In what ways do I support a system of justice? Justice—on the inside of us—is our willingness to become involved when some other person's right to life and growth is being violated. To fight only when our own existence is constricted or threatened is not yet a mature morality. Underlying this willingness to stand with others against the oppressor is a feeling that we are all in this together; 'we are members one of another.' And when fundamental rights are

---

[58] by Martin Niemoller (1892-1984), German Protestant pastor, social activist and Nazi prisoner in a concentration camp. From Wikiquote.

denied to any person, by just so much are the structures of human dignity and inclusiveness weakened for all of us.

EACH IS EVERYONE

Could be in the vast scheme of things

When all is said and done

That I am you, and you are me

And each is everyone.

The Planetary Community

Each is everyone and we all live in the same place—planet Earth. Both the green movement and global warming are ascending as a planetary force. The tragic environmental devastation predicted is the number one threat facing us today. Yet it wields little political power with the electorate. Surely no one has stated the commitment to the land more eloquently than Chief Sealth, for whom Seattle is named.

In a letter he wrote to President Franklin Pierce in 1855, the Chief expressed his puzzlement about the strange idea of buying land. To him, the earth appeared to be the white man's enemy rather than his brother or sister. In his famous 1854 speech, Chief Sealth said:

There was a time when our people covered the land as the waves of a wind-ruffled sea covered its shell-paved floor, but that time long since passed away with the greatness of tribes that are now but a mournful memory...

Our dead never forget the beautiful world that gave them being. They still love its verdant valleys, its murmuring rivers, its magnificent mountains, sequestered vales and verdant-lined lakes and bays, and ever yearn in tender, fond affection over lonely-hearted living, and often return from the Happy Hunting Ground to visit, guide, console and comfort them...

Every part of this soil is sacred in the estimation of my people. Every hillside, every valley, every plain and grove, has been hallowed by some sad or happy event in days long vanished. Even the rocks, which seem to be dumb and dead as they swelter in the sun along the silent shore, thrill with memories of stirring events connected with the lives of my people, and the very dust upon which you now stand responds more lovingly to their footsteps than to yours, because it is rich with the blood of our ancestors and our bare feet are conscious of the sympathetic touch. Our departed braves, fond mothers, glad, happy-hearted maidens, and even our little children who lived here and rejoiced here for a brief season still love these somber solitudes and at eventide they greet shadowy returning spirits. And when the last Red Man shall have perished, and when the memory of my tribe shall have become a myth among the White Men, these shores will swarm with the invisible dead of my tribe, and when your children's children think themselves alone in the field, the store, the shop, upon the highway or in the silence of the pathless woods, they will not be alone. In all the earth there is no place dedicated to solitude. At night when the streets of your cities and villages are silent and you think them deserted, they will throng with the returning hosts that once filled them and still love this beautiful land....

How is the world doing? My beloved nephew, Gregory Crosby (referenced in the book, *Living Kindness*, [see Bibliography] for his comparison of Amish and Las Vegas cultures), called me from the U.N. with this quote. "There are 2.4 billion people, more than a third of the world's population who do not have access to proper sanitation. More then 2.2 million people, mostly in developing countries, die each year from diseases associated with poor water and sanitary conditions."[59]

It is sobering to me to wonder how far the cost of war in Iraq for one year diverted to this cause would go to eradicate this problem world wide.

On The Commitment to Commitment

The morality of commitment is the structure of life—even though it makes life tough at times. It enables and accompanies the morality of authenticity. Inevitably, life brings us to face:

"What authority do I recognize

Other than, I want?

Whom do I serve other than myself?

What future am I helping

To bring off?"[60]

Commitment is risk-taking. It is not about being sure. It is about taking a stand. It is about making choices in a non-black-and-white world, where the final answer is rarely known for sure. It is about having the courage to be wrong, the courage to fail.

It is about making choices to establish one's direction rather than being dictated to by vacillating emotions or by an authority outside of self (or an inspired book interpreted by the authorities) or by the secondhand learnings of childhood.

4. The Core Morality Of Being My Word

When my words and action do not match, what is the other person to believe? When my words say "Thank you" in a sarcastic tone, would anyone believe that I am thankful?

---

59 U.N. Chronicle. Power of Water Issue, March 2003.
60 Ross Snyder

In the evolution of the species, we observed the natural order and related to each other and to nature before we had language. Language is the external expression of inward sensing, intuiting, and knowing. How desperately we grasp for words to say what resides in our deepest selves and what, profoundly, cannot be said. That grasping is highlighted when we try to communicate with someone who speaks a language foreign to our own.

Since all language is interpretation; therefore, all creeds and beliefs are interpretations. All myths, in their imaginative mystery, are interpretations. All poetry and prose, all historic embellishments and all revelations, are interpretive. How exciting is the pursuit of their essence! A core morality for the individual striving for authenticity is to find those words most congruent with one's own being and to know that one's words are *always being interpreted.*

What does it mean, then, to give one's word? First, we should understand that we create our word. Some ancients believed that the world was created with a word spoken. To *be* one's word is to be congruent. It is as if I am announcing to others: "You can count on me. My word is not idle. What I say I am creating. What I say is my being." Kierkegaard, the Danish existentialist, tells us that "the truth consists not in knowing the truth but in being the truth."

So when I say, "Thank you," in a sarcastic way, it is clear that I am not *being* my word. Look for consistency between what I say and what I do. Tell me when you perceive those inconsistencies that *will* be there. Because language is interpretive, there will often be a gap between what I mean and what you think I mean. Your feedback to me about that perceived gap is critical to us if we are to grow in our relationship.

Language creates reality. When an adult female refers to herself as a *girl*, she is creating within herself and her environment a way of being vastly different than when she says *woman* in referring to herself and other females. When organization leaders use the language of "men and girls" rather than "men and women" they are creating a different reality about how people will interact and about the career possibilities available.

Also, I am my word about commitment. If my words are:

Probably

Hopefully

If I can

I'll try

It wasn't my fault

Nobody told me

… then I create the likelihood of not achieving, of blaming, and finding excuses. If my words are:

I'll handle that

You can count on me

I'll complete it by (when)

… then I will create the likelihood of dependability and responsibility. Essentially, then, I will face the world as one whose word is truth.[61]

---

[61] These core morality essays are from the book *Living with Purpose When the Gods are Gone* by the author.

CHAPTER ELEVEN: LIFE'S LITTLE LESSONS

Only a few dozen residents live year round at the Castle Volpaia. I write this seated at Caffé Bar-Ucci, behind the fountain where I refresh myself each morning after my two kilometer walk up the hill on an ancient (I like to think) Roman road. I look up and see the church built centuries ago. To its right is a shaded restaurant overlooking the cypresses, olive trees, vineyards and forests that grace this paradise.

Paola Barucci (yes, of Bar–Ucci), the owner and waitress, is attentive to my needs for *acqua naturale* and *caffé*. I like it that, contrary to larger Italian cities, I can order "un caffe" without adding the word "espresso" and get what I call real Italian coffee!

As I drink my *caffé* and write this I face the ancient church and the shaded restaurant La Bottega (licensed in 1708) where older sister Carla creates exquisite Chianti dishes. Papa Oriano produces salami and vegetables, and Mama Gina is a strong presence in the square. She prepares the homemade-pasta and the *ribollita* and other exceptional dishes. Ombre, the spaniel, and Pallina, the part lab, brighten the lives of all who wander into this Barucci family world.

A line in the Barucci family brochure that I love is "Living simple moments in full consciousness means to render them unforgettable in future memories." Taking their advice, I stay present to the *caffé*, the fountain, the olive trees, the vineyards, and the constant arrival of tourists by foot, bikes and various motorized vehicles.

Giuliana and Enis Vergelli advertise *miele* (honey) on the door of their home, two hundred feet from the Castle. A purchase from their Podere Vergelli is an important social event. It includes a seat at their kitchen table, a glass of *Vin Santo, vino rosso,* or their *lemon-*

cello, along with conversation (they speak only Italian—Patricia and I only a little Italian) and perhaps singing. All of this is part of the purchase of two jars of world class *castagne* (chestnut) honey. Actually, Giuliana says "*castagne miste*" (chestnut mixed with other honey) since the bees do stray a bit from chestnut trees that populate the Chianti forest—the same trees that before the blight 100 years ago graced the eastern forests of the U.S.

Ritual and Meaning

My morning walk to Volpaia and my regular appointment with the *caffé* and the fountain and the Barucci's are ways that I create rituals in my life. In Seattle, it's my daily walk to the coffee shop at Pike Place Market, greeting many market friends along the way, singing with folk song writer Jim Hinde, and settling down with my New York Times. I need some predictable, stabilizing daily events.

Here it is my morning walk to Volpaia. I write. I converse. Today, with Australians, yesterday a young German hiking from Florence to Siena and days before with French hikers, American cyclists and Canadians, Dutch, Brits, Israelis and Italians!

On the journey up the hill, I meet and pet a cat that I have decided is the fourth reincarnation of our cat Skeezik which we lost years ago. A cathedral of green surrounds me on my walk. The blackberries are ripe—the grapes a month from harvest but already refreshing. The olives are maturing.

Today I remembered two mentors in my life. L. B. Sharp taught me to look beyond the botanical name. I reflect his teaching in my poem below and regularly honor his memory as I walk and "look beyond the name of yonder tree."

With Melvin Moody I discovered and learned to love the woods around Camp Wanake (Ohio) and especially the mother tulip tree. This past May, once again, I hugged the tree. It's not an easy task since it must be twelve feet around. I also hugged it for

Melvin and scattered some of his ashes at its base. With the insight from modern scientific knowledge I realize that I exchanged molecules, merging parts of the tree, my mentor and me as well as family members who were present. It was a satisfying ceremony.

I create rituals. I honor ancient rituals. But those that are part of our religious practice are often said to have become old and encrusted with decay and no longer useful or relevant. I think that happens when we get stuck in secondhand thinking about ceremonies and customs and forget the deeper meanings they have. In my daily walks—in Volpaia or Seattle—the rituals that surround the *caffè* or the espresso point to a deeper place in me, and I am drawn always to look through them to the deeper meaning.

L. B. Sharp

What is the name

Of yonder tree?

It has no name but this

That it has bark with furrows deep

And leaves with valleys green.

Gold blossoms grace the limbs in spring

And roots take hold unseen

Midst myriads of teeming life

Where miracles abound

A web that's only dimly known

Yet fortifies the ground

So those who ask "What is the name?"

Can breathe and drink and live!

To KNOW the tree—caress the trunk,

The leaf, the soil, and give

> But passing fancy to the words
>
> Assigned in this great game
>
> Lest we forget that all of life
>
> Is deeper than its name!

The Meaning of Life

What about deeper meanings in life? If life is a mystery, is there still meaning? Absolutely! Finding meaning is one of the mysteries to be solved. The first secret in solving it is to realize that the answer does not lie "out there" but "in here"—that is, inside yourself.

The second secret is that the meaning is constantly shifting—opening up like a flower in bloom. You create your own meaning and throughout your life you will constantly re-create it with a renewed enthusiasm. It is said that when King Arthur sent his knights on the quest for the Holy Grail, he told them to enter the forest where no one had gone before—that is, create a new path.

Meaning(s) lies within you. That's the journey. This is beautifully expressed in one of my favorite poems, by Joseph Campbell:

> The privilege of a lifetime is being
>
> who you are.
>
> The goal of the hero trip
>
> down to the jewel point
>
> is to find those levels in the psyche
>
> that open, open, open,
>
> and finally open to the mystery
>
> of your Self
>
> being Buddha consciousness
>
> or the Christ.
>
> That's the journey.

What does Campbell mean when he writes "being Buddha consciousness or the Christ"? First, let me restate my understanding of the simple core of Hinduism (from reading translations of the oldest recorded scriptures—The Upanishads). The highest deity is Brahma. But Brahma does *not* exist! Brahma is existence *constantly expanding*! You and I are one with that existence. Within each of us is Atman or Self. Atman and Brahma are of the same substance. You and I are one with Existence—sigh and realize the peace and beauty that comes with such knowing. You cannot *think* your way into this realization. Experiencing this Oneness is an intuitive act. So realizing the Buddha within us or Christ (Christos) within us is to discover our oneness with existence—with creation—with life!

The Gospel of John in the Christian New Testament begins by stating that the wisdom that was present in the beginning of time "became flesh"—became a person and "walked among us." John wrote that this person was Jesus of Nazareth to whom he applied the ancient word "Christos." Thus, some say Jesus the Christ or Jesus Christ not as a last name but as a designation of a unique role in history.

It is said that Jesus said, "I and the Father are one!" For several centuries Christians debated passionately whether that phrase applied only to Jesus or to all of us. Can we all say (as would the Hindus), "I and the highest deity are one" or is this reserved for Jesus only?

Finally, under pressure from Roman emperors who needed unity in the declining empire, the orthodox won and the free intuitive experiential thinkers lost. The survival of Christianity was at stake. To preserve unity you must enforce orthodoxy. Heresy (meaning free-thinking) is too unstable and unpredictable if an institution like the church is to survive.

Still, the church was confused. So they developed a doctrine (the Trinity) which included the belief that the Holy Spirit (of the three parts of the deity, with God the Father and the Son) could be present in each of us. So in his poem, Campbell is stating that you and I can eventually recognize ourselves as Christos, and as the Buddha.

There is an old saying, "If you meet the Buddha on the road, kill him!" That is, the Buddha is "in here," not "out there," so if you see or meet him, it must be an illusion! The Buddha is within each of us. As is Brahma. As is the Christos. As is Sophia (wisdom).

Meet them and embrace your deepest meaning.

The Meaning of Death

When one embraces the meaning and the mystery of life, acknowledging that there is no single answer, then one has died to the need for certainty. Alan Watts titled one of his remarkable books *The Wisdom of Insecurity*. Exactly! Life is insecure. Watts writes, "Nothing is more creative than death, since it is the whole secret of life. It means that the past must be abandoned, the unknown cannot be avoided. The 'I' cannot continue and that nothing can be ultimately fixed. When a man knows this, he lives for the first time in his life."

So why wait for physical death to discover these things? Death, defined as Watts has, is a twin of life. Don Juan, in Carlos Castenada's marvelous writings, tells Castenada to look over his left shoulder and see Death as a constant companion. Death is a reminder of the preciousness of each moment of life. Death is a reminder that "things fall apart"—all eventually is broken— and that insecurity is the reality of our existence. When something breaks or is lost, Patricia and I say to each other, "Of course," acknowledging that all is impermanent.

Embrace this and fear goes away. Of course, I'll eventually, sooner or later, lose my money, my things (my glasses!), my status, my ego, my consciousness. So, I celebrate this moment and know that fear will not change the future. Fear will only darken this moment.

I Always Walk Right Next to Death

I always walk right next to Death,

He's just a touch away,

He may reach o'er and take my breath

And end my mortal stay.

His presence need not morbid be

Nor need he be denied,

I simply brush reality

To know he's at my side.

Each moment then may be my last,

Each smile, each word, each deed,

If this be so then I can cast

Away my pretense need

That I be this or I be that

And I be who I'm not,

That I be who I think you'll like,

That I be who you thought.

If every moment of my life

Be this moment—no more,

Perhaps I then can choose to be

My truthful self, my core.

This death—he is my wise old self

My anchor in life's fray

I always walk right next to death,

He's just a touch away.

This became so clear one afternoon in Tuscany. Myriam, of DiVine Tours on Via Roma, who earlier had located our enchanting villa for us, helped us unravel the directions to a favorite winery. Carolyn, of Bar Dante had favored us by opening a fresh bottle of a local *vino rosso*. Later, relaxing, we sat at the center of Radda across from Porciatti Macelleria that provided such favorite treats as chopped chicken liver for *crostini, cipolline* onions in balsamic and olive oil, nutty-flavored pecorino cheese, marinated fresh anchovies, and an array of char-grilled vegetables in addition to the freshly butchered meats.

The church bells rang. Soon we saw a funeral procession led by the priest with dozens of women following, chanting over and over a prayer to Mary—a prayer to the feminine deity, a dimension missing for me in my Protestant up-bringing. And there was our friend Gina from Volpaia. Community! My heart reached out to her as she walked by, joining the women who were praying and the mix of men, women and children who followed the hearse bearing the departed one. Gina is only somewhat younger than I am. Someday they will walk for her and for other loved ones in her village, and for each of us someone will grieve.

The most tragic is for some one to die before "their time." My poem attempts to remind us both of a tragic aspect of war and our insensitivity.

COLLATERAL DAMAGE[62]

A little girl died today.

Collateral damage.

It's too bad she had to die.

Sometimes to save a village you must
destroy it.

The same with the little girl and her future
children.

---

[62] A phrase used by the military to indicate the deaths of non-military combatants. As I edit this book (November 10, 2004) I read that over 200 Iraqi civilians were killed this past week, mostly by insurgents but some from U.S. "surgical" strikes. A joint study by Johns Hopkins University and Al-Mustansiriya University in Baghdad estimated 100,000 more killed since the U.S. invasion than normally would have died in that period of time. New York Times, October 29, 2004. According to the Brookings Institute. the number of Iraqi citizens killed ranges from a possible 20,100 to 39,300. This was reported by the Associated Press in March 2005. Collateral damage is inevitable in war. Many armies conscientiously attempt to limit this and individual soldiers have acted heroically to protect civilians.

Too bad—collateral damage.

And oh—how did the Yankees do today?

The Stock Market—was it up or down?

What?

Collateral damage?

I already said it was a shame!

What else do you expect of me?

Loss

The task is to take any loss and turn it into wisdom. This is true for any mistake, any failure. We cannot, however, turn loss into wisdom by simply thinking about it differently. Rather, it requires that we grieve and then let go of the grieving, refusing to carry—for long—any guilt or anger and also refusing to fear that we will make new mistakes (we will). Otherwise, we are apt to let the loss become the central focus of our lives and be embittered and victimized by it.[63] Loss of a loved one, of health, of pride, or wealth—these are the seeds of wisdom.

The Meaning of Work

"So what are you? What do you do?" said the American to the Italian winemaker.[64] "I am a peasant," he said. Quickly and forcefully, the foreigner denied this. "You are not *just* a peasant," said the American. "I'm not *just* an owner," protested Paolo.

Quietly, this winemaker showed the stranger the label on his bottle which read, "...*Prodotto e imbottigliato dal coltivatore diretto Paolo Cianferoni*" ("Produced and bottled by peasant director Paolo Cianferoni"—also translated as "the director of cultivation"). But Paolo said "peasant."

He was quite proud. I have known this man for five years. He owns the land. He works in the fields. He crawls in the barrels. He

---

63 Inspired by reading Krishnamurti's *Freedom from the Known*.

64 Caparsa Winery, Radda in Chianti, Italy.

harvests (with help) and tenderly cares for his wine and olive oil. He produces and bottles and, at times, is the staff in his shop in Radda. His year 2000 vintage Doccio a Matteo received the highest (three glasses) rating in the authoritative wine guide, *Gambero Rosso* (2004).

He follows his bliss, his internal calling. The word vocation comes from the Latin word "calling." You are called from within to be a peasant or poet or whatever helps you to be *you*! Perhaps, unlike Paolo, you will find your bliss in something you don't do as a livelihood.

Even though my consulting and teaching has been an expression of my deepest self, I also have been singing at any time in any place, at the drop of a hat or a hint that, well, maybe a song would be nice, as long as I can remember. It is "who I am" in my ego-self. A singer. When I sing, I believe that I'm drinking from the well of my deeper real self. The pictures here and on the next page were taken, unknown to me, by Dario's assistant Ricardo, at Antica Macelleria, the Butcher Shop in Panzano (the most famous in Italy according to "Wine and Food Magazine") at the exact

This photo was taken at Antica Macelleria by Ricardo at the exact moment I opened my mouth to hit the highest tenor note in *Che Gelida Manina* from La Boheme.

moment I opened my mouth to hit the highest tenor note in *Che Gelida Manina* from La Boheme. Greatly encouraged by Dario Cecchini, the butcher, I had been singing along with the tenor on the C.D. I do know the Italian words. But the highest note is not mine to sing—nor has it ever been!

So the picture is a fake—that is, it is me opening my mouth on the one note I didn't sing! But the joy is not fake! Nor the enthusiasm! Nor Dario's enthusiasm, especially earlier when I sing along with Puccini's words:

Chi son?	Who am I?
Sono poeta.	I am a poet.
Che cosa faccio?	What do I do?
Scrivo.	I write.
E come vivo?	How do I live?
Vivo!	I live![65]

At "I live" an older employee and I raise both of our hands high celebrating the joy of life (of *vita!*) I hope that whatever your "work" is, it will be your bliss as well. I also find bliss in being a poet, a writer, a teacher, and a singer, and in the roles of husband, father, grandfather and great-grandfather! Each brings me joy in a different way. Each brings me bliss.

Bob and Dario at Antica Macelleria

---

[65] One English version translates *vivo* into "I survive." How insipid!

CHAPTER TWELVE:
A FEW TURNS IN THE SPIRITUAL ROAD

*A*s I sat on a rock in front of a sign reading "*Pruneto*" on the road to Volpaia, I made up a playful story about "creation." I have read and re-read various mythical accounts including the Biblical accounts with their majestic language—"and then there was light."

Being of a little more scientific bent, I began with … atoms.

Creation

At the very beginning there was only an atom—a super atom. Small as atoms go it was large enough to contain in it every energy and life-form that would ever exist.

It exploded!

Out came the fresh cold well water looking exactly like the well—or was it a spring from the side of the hill it snuggled against?—at my grandparents farm near Youngwood, Pennsylvania. As a child, mostly before my eighth birthday when we moved away, I would carefully open the door to the man-made cave that protected it. The coolness of the cave contrasted with the summer heat and was an invitation to drink the cold dark water at the west end of the cave. Large milk containers lined the walls. In this sanctuary I experienced awe mixed with fear in the dim light. How deep was the well? How safe was I within?

After the first explosion, another came, and the cave surrounding the well—the source/the womb—appeared. That was the second day of creation.

And then the first two humans opened their eyes in that cave that looked like my grandfather's cave. Curious and somewhat afraid, they opened the door. Instantaneously a corn field appeared to the east. To the south, a pigpen and a barn and to the north, a farmhouse and a garden. Above the cave to the west—an apple orchard.

After that, in each place where any of the humans directed their gaze, new creation occurred spontaneously. The creating occurred simply in the seeing! Each new creation became a new Garden of Eden. I bottled some water from the cave and went west. The cool water flows in Seattle where my cave and my current Garden of Eden embrace me.

That's my story of creation. With no mention of evolution, by the way. "Can one believe in evolution and be spiritual?" you may ask. Absolutely! And in much the same way that I can "believe in" the Biblical stories of creation and in the Big Bang theory and in my fantasy story as well.

In faith, you can believe in God and creation as traditionally defined and in evolution. I've had many devout Christian friends who believe in God as creator, and look to science (evolution) for the process. They see little conflict in this. That evolution and religion are *not* in conflict is supported in Catholic teaching (Pope Pius XII in 1950 and Pope John Paul in 1996). Evolutionary theory says nothing about the source or a "divine intelligence" guiding the process. These are theological issues. The scientific pursuit is about *how* life is continuously evolving, not about its Source.

In Hindu scriptures the highest deity is *constantly expanding* existence. The ten incarnations of Vishnu (one of the Hindu trinity) begin with Vishnu as a fish, then as a land creature (turtle) and later as half man and half animal. The incarnations tell of an evolution to the final, yet to come, tenth incarnation that leads to a last judgment day.

The first chapter of Genesis tells of a six-day creation with the creator resting on the seventh day—the Sabbath (Friday sundown to Saturday sundown). Many theologians see this as a sermon preached as Judaism evolved to emphasize Sabbath observance. After all, one of the Ten Commandments is to "Remember the Sabbath and keep it holy." Some fundamentalists take literally the six days, while other conservatives say it means six periods of time (i.e., God's "days" are longer). Some Christians (and all Jews and Muslims) worship on the Sabbath while many (including literalist) Christians worship on Sunday. The Hebrew creation stories (Genesis I is the seven-day story; Genesis 2–4 is the older Adam and Eve story) are a marvelous gift from the ancients. Creation stories from all the tribes and faiths of the world are to be celebrated.

Likewise, science. Evolution (the how) is its continuing gift.

Except for Christians who believe that (by their interpretation of the Bible) the earth is only about 6000 years old, there need be no conflict between evolution and faith.

Another question frequently asked in tracts handed out on street corners by devout fundamentalists is, "Are you saved?" Here's my take on that.

When I was ten I accepted an invitation from an evangelist (a guest preacher at our church) when she invited the people who were ready to accept Jesus to come to the front of the nave and kneel and be "saved." I was cleansed of all my sins. This is not a joke. Ten-year-old children may not have many or any dramatic sins, but in the eyes of fundamentalist/orthodox Christians, all of us are born sinners.

So, as defined by the elders kneeling around me, I was "saved" or "born again." And it was a very believable idea. I cried. I felt light and cleansed inside as if I had lost a few pounds. I felt ecstatic. I believed I had had a direct experience with God. I was special—set apart from my peers who had not yet been saved.

I am 77 years old as I publish this. I still feel warm inside when I recall that 10-year-old boy experience. I have many exquisite moments in my present life when I experience a oneness with existence. Clearly, I talk about it differently now. Maybe that's why I love and respect the ancient Hindu saying, "Truth is One, wise ones call it by many names." Now I think of salvation this way:

Salvation ...

is not a future event.
is not something you can think yourself into
is not a one-time only event
is not accompanied with any dogma
is not exclusive to any one religion
    or even to religion itself.
is not to save you from a bad future consequence.

Salvation ...

is about feeling cleansed right here, right now,
for now.
is foreign to your mind's insistence
    on continual bitterness
    or continual regret about the past
    or endless repetitive worry about the future.

Salvation ...

is to be grasped now without further thinking.
It could be as simple to say yes to as it would
be to drop a hot coal from your hands.

Realize your divinity,
Your oneness with the universe.
Just as you are.
...Now!

The deepest spirituality lies in the not-knowing, the ability to stay there, and the ability to say a resounding "yes" to life!

Many people believe that the place to go for this experience is a church, synagogue, mosque or other religious meeting place.

Going To Church

So the question is whether one truly can experience the indescribable there? Absolutely! But doing so is not simply a result of a particular kind of worship service. Rather, it's a result of a particular way of *being there*. So, the experience is largely up to *you*, not the externals of ritual or dogma.

On one brilliantly sunny Sunday, our friends Rita and Enrico took me to the Sant' Antimo Abbey which was tucked in a valley beneath the village Castelnuova. The first stone of the structure is said to have been laid in the eighth century.

The Gregorian Latin Mass was sung mostly by seven monks with occasional congregational response. The haunting unison notes and the sweet tenor solo tunes swirled through the six story high travertine alabaster stone cathedral. It was a feast for the ear and eyes, united with the touch of the stone, the permeating aroma of the incense and, for those choosing to participate, the taste of the wafer.

A sensate experience!

The service was in Latin and therefore not a "thinking" experience, except for those present who understood the words passionately delivered in the Italian sermon. For me the passion was engaging and enough.

The mystery of the Mass, a sensate and intuitive moment pointing beyond itself to the indescribable mystery, is awesome. Patricia and I have been in awe in a Russian Orthodox service in Moscow. The same sense of a mystery pointing beyond the enchanting experience of the moment was especially strong for me in the chanting of the priests and the visual beauty of the interior.

Unversed as I am in Islam, I imagine the same when I see Muslims kneeling for prayer, or walking at Mecca round and round the Kabah which their tradition says was built by Adam and then repaired/rebuilt by Abraham and his first born son (by Hagar) Isma'il.

Transcendent moments!

All religions have created such opportunities. As a boy I loved the gospel songs we sang in church. Yes, the words were sung in the language I knew, but it was something in the union of voices and the rhythms of the music that enchanted me. I still love singing gospel songs and spirituals, but if I were to take many of those words literally today, the experience of a-mystery-beyond would escape me.

In life a Jesus *happens*! A Moses *happens*! A Buddha, a Zoroaster, a Mohammed *happens*. Religions arise attempting to perpetuate the peak transcendent experiences of their first hero. They formulate orthodoxy or right-thinking. They often become rigid and dogmatic. In the midst of having to maintain the approved right beliefs, religions again and again lose that original spark. The mind and dogmas trump intuitive faith.

It doesn't have to be this way. We can have an experience of the mystery of life in a house of worship as long as we don't get stuck on the doctrines, the symbols, or the words. The mystery will rekindle as long as we don't let it—the indescribable experience that we each create—ever be defined for us by others or finally in a fixed way by ourselves. Definitions are limited. They are the enemies of awe and mystery.

Mary Magdalene

In yet another place, Patricia and I look upon traditional religious scenes and symbols and are moved with awe at deeper meanings. This time we are looking at the grand painting hanging on the wall space at the end of a room in the Museo Civico in Sansepolcro,

Italy. It is a scene of the Last Supper by an unknown artist of the 17th century, painted for the minor observant church which is now closed and *not* open for visitors. The church was built in 1560 or roughly a century before the painting adorned its wall. We stand before this painting, stunned by its beauty, even its existence, and its placement in this room!

Apparently recently refinished, the painting has a striking resemblance to Leonardo da Vinci's famous painting(s) of the same Last Supper. There are 13 at the table, mostly all facing the painter. Jesus is in the center. To his left (not right as in Leonardo da Vinci's rendition) sits the only unbearded person, with braided hair and a very feminine appearance. The title of the painting is "Suppressed Magdalene of the Minor Observant church" and is recorded on the sign describing the painting in both Italian and English. It is an intriguing title, and we eagerly turned our earphones to the appropriate English translation.

The voice says something like, "Now on the far wall in the next room you'll see a painting of the Last Supper. On the wall facing it…" Then began the customary long explanations of the other pictures in the room. Our friend Ted Hunter had done the same tour with a guide. He had a similar experience and noticed that questions about the painting were not answered!

Mary Magdalene is an important New Testament figure. According to the New Testament, she was at the crucifixion and was the first to "see" Jesus resurrected. She was, arguably, the one who anointed Jesus (one of the rare events mentioned in all four gospels.) She was close to Jesus. In the Gnostic Gospel of Philip (not chosen in later centuries as one of the "orthodox" scriptures) she is referred to as his companion "who he often kissed on the mouth." A strong tradition exists in southern France that she was his wife and bore Jesus' daughter, Sarah. Some claim she was, more than anyone, his successor.

In the sixth century Pope Gregory confused her with a woman of dubious reputation (prostitute?) mentioned in Luke 7:36-50. Modern scholars refute this. *No such reference to Mary Magdalene exists in the New Testament,* and yet many Christians hold that opinion today. I studied for four years in a Protestant seminary and held that opinion of her! The Pope's declaration was very influential.

So the "suppressed Magdelene" of the 17th century painting and the now closed church "of minor observants" was, once again (could I say), suppressed.

I am not a conspiracy theorist. I love hearing conspiracy stories but don't take them *too* seriously. *The Da Vinci Code* was an exciting mystery read for me, especially with its references to some of the Gnostic Gospels (Gospel of Mary [Magdelene], Thomas, Truth, Philip) which indeed *do* exist but were excluded from the New Testament as heretical or not orthodox (right-thinking.)

I have read these and enjoyed them. I've also seen a copy of da Vinci's *Last Supper* where the person to Jesus' right hand (where a wife would more likely sit) indeed could be a woman and, if so, is probably Mary Magdelene.

Margaret Starbird's scholarly books on the possibility of Jesus and Mary being married—and her possible role as the leader of the early church—are fascinating. Certainly there is strong suggestive evidence supporting this. These possibilities are profound and exciting to consider. For me, they increase the mystery. However, as she acknowledges, the historical evidence that Jesus was married and that this was suppressed is as circumstantial "as is the gospel account of the Passion ...(which is) parallel to the ancient life/death/resurrection cycles of the pagan gods Tammuz, Ba'al, Adonis, etc."[66]

There is no reference in the New Testament or anywhere else (including the Gnostic gospels) to Jesus being married, which was expected for both a man his age and a man called "Rabbi". It was

---

[66] Personal correspondence from Margaret Starbird.

also a long time before celibacy became formalized in the 12th century in the Roman Catholic Church, and therefore unlikely anyone would have deleted such references from the early writings for that reason. Also, despite the growing status of the Virgin Mary, the mother of Jesus, (after the stories first appeared in Matthew and Luke in A.D. 80-85) nobody deleted New Testament references to other children she bore—that is, to Jesus' siblings.

On the other hand it was (and is) widely believed in Provence (France) that Mary arrived with (Saint) Sarah in A.D. 42 and that Jesus "royal blood still flowed in the veins of the noble families of Provence ..."[67] Indeed, when the Christians captured Jerusalem in the first Crusade, Godfroi of Lorraine in France became the Baron of Jerusalem[68]. He was believed to be a descendant of Jesus through Sarah.

> "Sarah" means princess in Hebrew, so I'm inclined to believe that the child was a daughter. The surviving written versions of the oral legends mention a "servant girl" named Sarah, but they were written by Churchmen in the 13th century...so of course, they would have to conform to "doctrine" to avoid confrontation with the Inquisition. My "take" is that the child on the boat was a "princess from a far away land" ("Sarah").[69]

Jesus' alleged marriage to Mary called "the Magdalene" may have been kept secret – not mentioned – because of the extreme danger to Mary and Sarah following the crucifixion. If Jesus was crucified (a Roman method of execution) for sedition – that is for being suspected as one who would attempt the overthrow of the Romans, then his wife and child would have been in grave danger.

What matters—beyond the mystery—is the role of the feminine in my life. If suppressed, my compassion will be missing.

---

[67] Margaret Starbird. *The Woman with the Alabaster Jar.* p. 70
[68] Ibid
[69] Personal correspondence from Margaret Starbird.

Religion without compassion is at the animal level. It creates enemies and foments wars. It is about power and conquest. Without compassion for all life, without the grasp of my oneness with mother earth and with existence—in short, without the feminine principle—not simply Mary Magdalene but the feminine in all of us is suppressed.

CHAPTER THIRTEEN: BEING THERE

*A*t lunch in Panzano, at a table overlooking thousands of acres of breath-taking Tuscan landscape, four Americans were seated next to us about midway through our meal. Unfortunately, one of them had an unusually loud voice and did most of the talking. It was like she was the guest speaker. I wouldn't have minded so much if she had not been speaking in English, if, instead, she had been speaking in any language I didn't understand.

Patricia and I would then have commented on how beautiful the cadence of her speaking was, and we would have found it easy to continue our conversation. However, the problem was not only that we understood her language; after all, she might have been a truly engaging speaker describing her adventures in some exotic place. But she wasn't and she didn't, and so in both content and volume the conversation at the next table intruded on our otherwise lovely evening.

Here's the picture: A most scenic setting. Exquisite food. Chianti wine. An enchanting town (Panzano). And here were these people talking not about the setting, food or wine; not about their Tuscan experience, not about being with each other but about things that had happened to them in Chicago and Florida! If were to follow them to Chicago, I would probably hear them describe their memories of this lunch in Tuscany.

What was so engaging about what happened last week in Chicago? How could these four people apparently fail to notice the moment, experience this place and these companions—in the here and now?

Even as I write this at Bar-Ucci, a group arrives. They have been at Castle Volpaia for 15 minutes, and they are now talking about next week's trip north to Piedmont. They say nothing about here, about now, about the present moment. Nothing about the

Castle that sits 30 feet from us. Nothing about the Volpaia Chianti wines from grapes surrounding us. Nothing about our amazing waitress or the fountain or the piazza or the Italian coffee.

Are triangles so deeply embedded in human experience that we must continually be here but talk about there, be with each other but talk about someone else? Have we lost the capacity to be fully aware in this moment—here, now?

BY LOOKING INTO THE PAST

To visit Emily Dickinson
Sip wine with Paul Cezanne
A café on a cobbled street
Passion, fire, élan.

To vibrate in their special space
And live my fantasy
'mid rumors of the world they knew,
A moment just for me.

I'd listen with a special ear,
My eyes would watch with care,
I'd drink in every single word —
An honor to be there.

But so few went to Emily—
Cezanne, he was alone,
Suppose by looking to the past
We miss our very own!

I can walk in your living room
And have a cup of tea
Then drink in all the gift that's you
While you can feast on me.

The Value of Being Present … to Doing "Nothing"

Patricia and I often take turns reading a few favorite pages we've read or written today. We don't watch TV in Europe. We read, write, sing, sleep, eat, drink the wine of the vicinity, visit nearby villages, shop (mostly for food and wine) cook (her task and joy) clean-up (my task and not-as-yet much joy), wash clothes and hang them up to dry in the magnificent Tuscan sun (guess who), pick a tomato or two (me), select the *vino* for the meal (guess who), watch the sunset, walk (mostly me each morning to Volpaia), view the fields and forests. And pause.

The other day Patricia was reading (again) in Francis Maye's *Bella Tuscany,* and now because of her own experience of Tuscany, she more fully understood the phrase: "*Dolce far niente.*" "The sweetness of doing nothing," which Maye learned from her Tuscan friends. For me, "doing nothing" is sweet when I am not programmed into a pressing daily agenda, and am able to be fully present when doing the activities I just mentioned (i.e., hanging up clothes, selecting the wine).

In Tuscany, we were reminded of the deep pleasure of doing or planning nothing, that is, of being in the present. When our minds turn instead to the future or the past, we miss this very moment!

I am learning to turn my mind off when I frantically begin to fear what isn't here yet, to worry about what was and can't be changed, or to review a bitterness about something in the past that I won't forgive myself or another for.

The past does not exist: The future never arrives as "future" but only as the "present'—the now—the fleeting now. How may I create "stillness" in my life in order to experience it as it happens? *Dolce far niente.*

Expecting What Isn't

Sitting again in the *caffè*, I remember an experience in an Italian restaurant in the U.S. There was a round table next to mine set for six. I wondered how many would be seated there and guessed five, and I was fearful that one would talk too loudly. As mentioned earlier, it seemed to me that in otherwise quiet restaurants someone is chosen to speak as if all the room needed to hear his message. I wondered, "How will I cope?"

So, I sat in that restaurant, fearing a future that had not yet come, stimulated by some negative memories from my past of events that were actually quite rare. And I thought, "What am I doing to myself?"

I was blinded by those fears to the immediate moment. Then, as I remember it, something brought me back to the scene before me, to that particular moment, to the now/now/now. And I remember asking myself, "Did you come to your favorite spot to not be present to it or, rather, to be present only to your feelings of fear?" I remember noticing then the smile from my favorite waiter, the candlelight set against a backdrop of soft autumn sun fading into evening, my favorite dish, Ella singing as only Ella can, the deep purple black-cherry-scented wine. Ah!

That evening I recognized something very important: that I could choose what I wished to be present to. I smile, sitting here in this entirely Italian place today—an Italian *caffè* in Italy!—as I think about what I might have missed that night had I stayed in my fear and anxiety. The answer is pretty simple: I would have missed truly being there!

Est! I only exist in the present moment. The future never comes—only the "now" keeps arriving. The past is my unique personal illusion. Alan Watts[70] speaks of the "spoiler of the present.... The power of memories and expectations is such that for most

---

[70] In *The Wisdom of Insecurity*.

human beings the past and the future are not *as* real, but *more* real than the present. The present cannot (for most people) be lived happily unless the past has been 'cleared up' and the future is bright with promise." Hell is to live in constant reference to an anticipated future. Hell is to believe that my present is determined by my past Hell is to sit in that lovely restaurant as dusk approached and worry about the unpleasant group that may soon be seated next to me and ruin my peace of mind with their loud talking. Hell is to believe that my peace is dependent on how others behave. I didn't need to wait for this event to disrupt my peace of mind. I had succeeded in doing so all by myself!

As I thanked my waiter that night, I flowed in and out of both fear of the future and peace in the moment—twins—one prominent for (too many) moments and then the other—a better choice. I remember now that as I rose to leave, I noticed that no one had been seated at the round table—except in my fantasy.

In the *Joseph Campbell Companion*, which is absolutely one of my favorite books and which I have read and reread, he tells a story about an experience with Alan Watts whose books I have also read and reread! Two of my (unmet) mentors in one story. What could be better!

Campbell is in New York City, impatiently waiting for his wife who is later than expected. Alan Watts says to him, "You're expecting what isn't." Immediately Campbell begins seeing and hearing what is, and indeed there is much to see, hear, touch, taste, and smell on any corner in New York—In fact, anywhere. Everywhere. Be here now! Expect what is! *That's the beginning of wisdom.*

In that wonderful story where Moses is sent (by "God") to go to Egypt to free the Hebrew slaves, Moses asks the voice the name of the one whose voice is sending him on such a mission.

SAID MOSES TO THE VOICE
(Of God, Yahweh, Jehovah, Allah, Allaha)

What's your name?

"I am that I am.

Look it up (Exodus 3:14).

Or, I am becoming what I am becoming"

Tell them that "I am that I am" sent you

Strange name. But:

A wonderful name for deity.

"I am being—in process."
  Aren't we all?

Uniquely unfinished is the rest of my story—our story.

To begin each day in wonder and amazement.

To drop yesterday's sorrow, bitterness, frustration.

To die to the past.

We are only alive in this moment.

No other moment exists.

My name is "I am becoming who I am becoming."

I honor my past—my culture—my childhood faith.

But, "…life is too short to have just one identity"[71]

And I move on.

A new day keeps dawning.

What's your name?

The Wine, The Place

Amidst the heavenly, intense electrical energy of a storm one evening, Georgio drove his car up the driveway. We had often said "*Sera,*" short for "*Buona sera*" or "Good evening," but never before had he wandered so close to our rotunda—the magical circle outside our villa where a 300-year-old mulberry tree reigns supreme and dispenses wisdom.

---

[71] Don Juan (of Carlos Castaneda) speaking of his parents who had died "tragically because they could not let go of their desire for revenge against their Mexican prosecutors. He said that they lived and died like American Indians without realizing above all, that life is too short to have just one identity." From Mindel's book, *The Shaman's Body.* p. 50

Rita and Enrico Tanzini, the owners of our villa, had spoken of his wine-making ability. The problem, as we soon would read on his label, was that he made it for "migliori amici." It is a wine made, not for money, but with love for "best friends".

One of our few goals on this trip was to drink wine from the vines surrounding us. To look at a vine abundant with grapes nearly ready for harvest and then to drink the wine made from that actual field is a deep thrill to me. Rita and Enrico have shared Giovanni's (Rita's father) outstanding wine made from grapes bordering the northwestern side of the villa.

My dad's generation worked the fields, milked the cows, gathered the eggs. My generation had its gardens when possible, bought food from the store, had milk delivered until that practice stopped, and bought our eggs by the dozen. I hear stories that many in the current generation don't know where milk and eggs come from.

This separation from our source, from our place, is a huge loss. Enter Georgio who like many others in Tuscany co-creates with Mother Nature the essentials that grace their tables every day. He stepped from his car and beckoned us to follow him. "*Adesso—now?*" I asked hopefully. "*Si,*" he replied.

Soon we were seated in an underground room where the stone walls and arches all bore his mark. Sketches of the very constellations we watched each evening spread across his walls—his sketches—his paintings—and yes, the wine.

Ah, the wine. The wine of Massima and Georgio Finocchi—for friends only. For this shining event, we are included!

GEORGIO'S TREAT

Now I know that when
I'm near the vine
The wine seems

always right.

And some may think I'm

Too inclined

To rate it "out of sight."

But Georgio's treat

Excuse me please

I've tasted grapes before.

I know that when my

Eyes light up

Patricia's eyes meet mine.

The moment's here—embrace it now

Don't miss each sip of wine.

In moments like these, one is encouraged, by the richness of the experience, to be *fully present*. Patricia and I breathed in the place, the wine, our new friend. We sit in this exquisite room created by Georgio and Massima. Georgio speaks *only* Italian. We speak little Italian, yet conversation flowed. The wine is served with biscuits and Beethoven.

Then we were invited to pour for ourselves the new wine straight from the vat of the 2003 vintage! Soon it will begin its life in the French *bariques* (oak barrels), ready for drinking a few years later. I cannot describe what a thrill it was for us to turn the spout ourselves. The wine was served in long-stemmed *bellisimi* shaped crystal glass. "The glass is everything," he explained, or so we believed. "Wine is like a woman," he said as he lightly touched Patricia's shoulder, "It takes aging to be appreciated."

Finally, we were offered the lemoncello, made, as he carefully said, from a formula. Yes, we said, but we reminded him that it takes a good chemist to follow a formula and an artist to create everything that went into this gracious evening.

As we walked out into the evening, I was again filled with the wholeness of the moment. The wine was now only a recent memory but the night beckoned as Patricia and I stopped at the rotunda where earlier we had observed our evening ritual:

Our Ritual Each Evening Between 7:00 And 7:30 PM

> The sun sets
>
> And the earth moves.
>
> The bat brigades swoop over our villa and
>> into the vines,
>
> Feasting all the while.
>
> We welcome them.
>
> This moment will never
>
> happen again.
>
> This sunset will never
>
> happen again.
>
> Seize the moment!
>
> *Tat Tvam Asi*

CHAPTER FOURTEEN:
Arrivederci, CHIANTI

LAST NIGHT

Last night we sat on the rotunda outside
 our villa

near Radda.

We watched an electrical storm.

Tat Tvam Asi.

Tat Tvam Asi. Yes, we have become one with this place. As we prepare to return to Seattle, I become even more present to being here in Chianti, as though if I look hard and long enough at the fields and sky and vines or listen fully enough to the sounds of Verdi carried on the breeze or inhale deeply enough the scented air or taste fully enough the wine at dinner, I can fix this place in my memory and create a new richness in our home in Seattle.

If I were a photographer, these pictures in my mind's eye would grace the pages of this book, pictures of everyone we encountered—of Diego at Carpaccio, Nicola at La Caravella, Maurizio at Easy-Venice Tours, Pino at Trattoria Ai Tre Ponti, Michela on her clarinet and Roberto playing his bass with the other musicians near the Basilica San Marco. We would also feature our dear friend Sylvia and our many friends from the Alcoa Fusina plant near Venice.

In Chianti, there would be Micol at Bar-Ucci, Vito at Volpaia Osteria, and Miranda, near Radda, whose *ravioli tartufi* comes with *her* sliced truffles on *her* home-made pasta which is served with *her* olive oil and bread, and again, *her* primo wine. *Vita!*

Truly our cuisine experience is deeply enriched by our visits to Badia a Coltibuono and to Osteria del Castello in the parks of

Castello di Brolio where Chef Seamus O'Kelly creates exquisite culinary experiences.

And there would be a picture of the blue purple grapes about to be harvested. My photograph would show the abundant fullness and rich hues of cluster after cluster of these dark skinned beauties on vine after vine. Then in a world class photo, I would show all the various shades of green surrounding the clusters—the silvery olive leaves, the deep green cypresses and the shaded forest in the background.

In this serene world I would allow myself one recording to accompany my pictures. Late each evening, the canine chorus begins. From the distant northeast hills, first one soprano and then dozens of others begin the nightly concert. Soon, from the hills to our west, a lone bass is joined by many others who, I'm sure, eagerly wait each evening to serenade us in the valley—at least those of us who have stayed awake long enough to be enchanted by this *a cappella* barking choir. And then, from the southeast comes one tenor and then many other tenors, singing their version of Donizetti, Puccini, Rossini, and, ah, yes, now I hear one of those engaging Verdi choruses. It is one more time of magic, gifted to Patricia and me as we sit by our mulberry tree under a brilliant starlit sky. Who could ask for anything more? We look at each other—smile deeply—and laugh with joy!

This is an enchanted and enchanting place. I've always loved the lines in Camelot when Arthur is singing to Guinevere about the laws in Camelot—never raining or snowing at inconvenient times. This must be Camelot. By ancient law, the land in Chianti must remain about 75% forest, and this seems to be the case as far as my eyes can see.

Even in its ecosystem, the place is Camelot-like perfect. There is the rare mosquito and a few flies. More would be unlikely since the birds in this balanced ecology and the bat brigades at night manage what in my country takes insecticides, except for exceptional farmers who know how to use "organic" processes to co-create with Mother Nature.

Chianti

Surprised was I today to hear

Lone humming in my ear.

How could this be, in Chianti

Where laws from yesteryear

Declared the forests would remain

The queen of this fair place.

Where even grapes and olive trees

Exist in humbler space.

Mosquito, travel home with me

To my sweet land of liberty

And, sad for me, but good for you

You'll find a lot of family.

Now as we prepare to return to our "sweet land of liberty," I know that I shall return to this place. We spend our last night at Carla's LaBottego in Volpaia, and with sadness we set out to celebrate both our joy for this special month and our pain in leaving.

La Bottego has an outdoor garden with a stunning view, but tonight it is too cold to do that. On the street level floor there is a grocery store-like room with a few tables which are not set for dining. Yes, the answer quickly comes, we can eat here!

With great pleasure we settle down in the far corner near the telephone and the postcards set out for tourist appeal. Above us are the racks of mostly local wines.

At the next table there are some English-speaking people (Americans) drinking wine. We will be with Americans soon enough, we think, and wish that, if there must be others at the next table, that they be soft-spoken Europeans conversing lilting French or robust German or romantic Italian. We are fussy about these evening meals which contain such ceremony and ritual for us like the opening of the wine, and the dipping of bread in the fragrant olive oil. So, we hope they will speak in low tones, and soon depart—both of which they did.

About 15 minutes later a middle-aged man who had earlier been with the American group was suddenly standing in front of me. As I looked up, he said, "Excuse me, is your name Bill?"

"Close enough" said Patricia, "It's Bob."

"Did you teach...? My name is Steve Tighe."

Instantly I recalled this man whom I had known as a student 27 years ago. I spelled his name correctly to indicate recognition. My emotional memory of warmth kicked into gear. He had been a "special" student/person in my life for that brief period.

On August 1, 1977 a classmate of his named Jim Clarke met and invited Patricia (my wife) to a closing songfest led by me to celebrate the end of a six-week residential summer school program. Steve remembered Patricia being there with Jim, and it was on that day (her 40th birthday) that she and I saw each other for the first time. (But we didn't meet.)

After we reminisced about this experience, Steve went back upstairs. Later, a woman named Cindy invited us to come upstairs and asked me to surprise him by singing "Happy Birthday". I agreed. My performance led to more wine and reminiscing, more singing—more joy. But above all, the evening gave us a unique connective moment that was enhanced by a 27-year long invisible, golden thread.

Just before leaving, I chose to sing the last words of Donizetti's *Una Furtiva Lacrima* (One Furtive Tear):

Cielo, si può morir (Heaven, I could die),

Di più non chiedo (I could ask for nothing more).

I looked Steve in the eyes as I sang.

Arrivederci, Steve.

Arrivederci, Volpaia.

ARRIVEDERCI

Good-bye

It's simple—Simply Now—eternal

Accepted

Peace

A deep breath

A sigh

Life remains a mystery

That's what is.

Expect what is.

That's where wisdom lies.

That's the simple truth.

Freed from second-hand frantic answers.

Freed from second-hand.

Freed.

Chapter Fourteen: Arrivederci, Chianti

AFTERWORD

$\mathcal{A}$s stated in the acknowledgements, in June 2004 a friend suggested that I write another book.

In June 1904 my beloved Grandfather Erwin began writing a book. He completed it by 1906 and published it in 1926 two years before I was born.

I loved my grandfather. As a small boy I would sit beside him in "his" pew at the United Brethren Church (a mainline Protestant denomination that today is merged with the United Methodists). I remember him as a gentle, loving, and devout man. He was the patriarch and spiritual leader of our family.

In the 1920s, according to my mother, he and the pastor who baptized me started a Ku Klux Klan chapter in our small town in Pennsylvania. The Klan was strong in the North in the '20s.

These two pictures of this man are hard to reconcile: my devout Grandfather, author of "Twenty Pathways Leading to Judgment" (one of these being "prejudice") organizing a Klan chapter with its anti-Black, anti-Catholic and anti-Jewish agenda.

As reference earlier, my parents became so ashamed of this part of our history that they wanted it kept secret. But the past must be acknowledged. If we deny the "dark side" of our heritage we may relive it—we may embody it again! We may cross that "thin line" that I write about in Chapter 5. Further, if we deny our own dark side we will never understand the dark side of others.

During World War II, many Christians supported the anti-Semitism of Hitler's government. Many Christians today support bigotry towards those of other religions, skin colors, sexual orientation, culture, and on and on. Bigotry and prejudice have been with us since the beginning of time. They are not our natural endowments, but rather are viewpoints that are taught to us by others when we are very young.

But, as with all second-hand learning, they can be "unlearned," and we can be freed from the narrowness of those early life experiences. My parents revered my grandfather but were able to step beyond the restrictive teachings of the church and my grandfather's endorsement of the Klan. He, also, left the Klan after that brief, unfortunate experience.

As I, a hundred years later, write my spiritual book, I continue to feel blessed to have had a grandfather who thought and wrote about his spiritual wisdom, and parents who questioned the rightness of something like McCarthyism, and the little brown Klan book. May future generations say the same about their grandfather and their parents.

Selected Bibliography

Altman, Donald. *Living Kindness*. Makawao, Maui, HI: Inner Ocean Publishing Inc., 2003.

Ahmed, Akbar S. *Islam Today*. London, New York, NY: I.B. Publishers, 2002.

Armstrong, Karen. *Islam*. New York, NY: The Modern Library, 2000.

Armstrong, Karen. *The Battle for God*. New York, NY: Ballantine Books, 2000.

Campbell, Joseph. *Thou Art That*. Novato, CA: New World Library, 2001.

Campbell, Joseph. *The Inner Reaches of Outer Space*. Novato, CA: New World Library, 2002.

Douglas-Klotz, Neil. *Prayers of the Cosmos*. San Francisco, CA: HarperSanFrancisco, 1990.

Ehrman, Bart C., *Truth and fiction in The Code*. Oxford: Oxford University Press, 2004.

Hamilton, Adam. *Confronting the Controversies: Biblical Perspectives on Tough Issues*. Nashville, TN: Abingdon Press, 2005.

Jones, Rufus. *Some Exponents of Mystical Religion (1930)*. Whitefish, MT: Kessinger Publishing, 2003.

Journey of Man. PBS Home Video, 2003

King, Ursula. *Christian Mystics: The Spiritual Heart of the Christian Tradition*. New York, NY: Simon and Schuster, 1998.

Krishnamurti, Jiddu. *Freedom from the Known*. San Francisco, CA: HarperSanFrancisco, 1975.

Laughlin, Paul Alan. *Remedial Christianity*. Santa Rosa, CA: Polebridge Press, 2000.

Mayes, Frances. *Under the Tuscan Sun*. New York, NY: Broadway Books, 1997.

Merton, Thomas. *New Seeds of Contemplation*. Norfolk, CT. New Directions Publishing Corporation, 1962.

Mindell, Arnold. *The Shaman's Body*. San Francisco, CA: HarperSanFrancisco, 1993.

Nikhilananda, Swami. *The Upanishads.* Ramakrishna-Vivekananda Center, 17 E. 94th St., New York, N.Y. 10028, 1977.

Oxnam, G. Bromley. *I Protest.* Greenwood Press, 1979.

Osbon, Diane K., editor. *Reflections on the Art of Living: A Joseph Campbell Companion.* New York, NY: Harper Collins Publishers, 1991.

Pagels, Elaine. *Beyond Belief.* New York, NY: Random House, 2003.

Pennington, M. Basil. *Thomas Merton, My Brother.* Great Britain: New City Press, 1996.

Rowse, A.L. *Homosexuals in History.* New York, NY: Dorset Press, 1977.

Scherer, John. *Work and the Human Spirit.* Scherer Leadership Center, 1993. www.scherercenter.com.

Short, Ron. *Learning in Relationships: Foundation for Personal and Professional Success.* LIAT@learningingaction.com. 1998.

Starbird, Margaret. *The Woman with the Alabaster Jar.* Rochester, VE: Bear and Company Publishing, 1993

The Good Book of Love: Sex in the Bible. A & E Home Video, 2000.

Tillich, Paul. *Dynamics of Faith.* New York, NY: Perennial, 2001

Thurman, Howard. *Deep is the Hunger.* Richmond, IN: Friends United Press, 1973.

Thurman, Howard. *The Growing Edge.* Richmond, IN: Friends United Press, 1974.

Thurman, Howard. *With Head and Heart: The Autobiography of Howard Thurman.* New York, NY: Harvest/HBJ, 1981.

Thurman, Howard. *Meditations of the Heart.* Boston, MA: Beacon Press, 1999.

Tolle, Eckhart. *The Power of Now.* Novato, CA: New World Library, 1997.

The Torah: A Modern Commentary. Edited by W. G. Plant. New York, NY: By the Union of American Hebrew Congregations, 1981.

van Renterghem, Tony. *When Santa Was a Shaman.* St Paul, MN: Llewellyn Publications, 1995.

Wallen, John. (the original) *Interpersonal Gap.* by John Wallen. www.crosbyod.com

Wallen, John. *The Interpersonal Gap. Appendix O, in Walking the Empowerment Tightrope: Balancing Management Authority and Employee Influence.* by Robert P. Crosby. HRD Quarterly. OD&D Inc., King of Prussia, PA 19406, 1992.

Watts, Alan. *Myth and Religion.* Rutland, VE: Charles E. Tuttle Company, Inc., 1996.

Watts, Alan. *The Wisdom of Insecurity.* New York, NY: Random House, 1951.

Who Wrote the Bible? A & E Entertainment, 1996.

ABOUT THE AUTHOR

*B*orn in 1928, Robert Crosby spent his childhood in the Pittsburgh, Pennsylvania, area.

Impacted by the early T-Group process spawned by Kurt Lewin, the outdoor education movement of L.B. Sharp, and the world of mysticism inspired by being in the presence of Howard Thurman, he integrated these into his work.

The author has had several careers. He was ordained in the United Methodist Church in 1953 and, later, was on the national staff of that church. He holds a B.A. from Otterbein College and degrees from the United Theological Seminary (Master of Divinity), Boston University School of Theology (Master of Sacred Theology) and an honorary doctorate, Doctor of Humane Letters (LHD), from Bastyr University. He taught at Gonzaga University from 1969 to 1971. Also, he founded the Leadership Institute of Spokane (now Seattle) LIOS in 1969 and has taught in a Masters degree program since 1973, most recently at Martin University (named for Martin Luther King and St. Martin de Porres) in Indianapolis.

He and his wife Patricia reside in Seattle. They collectively have 10 children, 14 grandchildren, one god-grandchild in Ukraine, and one great-grandchild.

This is his sixth book.

OTHER BOOKS BY ROBERT P. CROSBY

LIVING WITH PURPOSE WHEN THE GODS ARE GONE

WALKING THE EMPOWERMENT TIGHTROPE:
Balancing Management Authority and Employee Influence

The Cross-Functional Workplace
Matrixed Project and Task Success

Cultural Change in Organizations
A Guide to Leadership and Bottom-Line Results

I ALWAYS WALK RIGHT NEXT TO DEATH
and Other Poems of Life

Poems
~~#4~~
~~127~~

(C) 152 Chianti* *By ancient law, the land in Chianti's ~~forest~~ must remain 75% forest.
~~134~~

146

(E) 154

(A) 149 Our Chianti evening ritual

    6 ONe
    8 OM
    9 Om ~~with footnote~~
    5 + par

(B) 147 Georgio's treat (our LaCapanna neighbor) *
            footnote - see underlined words

(D) At Cape Barucci (in Volpaia)

    A/B/C/D/E in sequence also

        Otelsa ~~Arbot~~ Venezia

    The Eternal Now at end
        preceded by
            5/6/8/9

146 after In Awe of Aging

CPSIA information can be obtained
at www.ICGtesting.com
Printed in the USA
FSHW02n0204140718
50244FS

9 780977 690008